John Comaroff was born in Cape Town in 1945. He obtained a BA degree at the University of Cape Town, then became a post-graduate student in social anthropology at the London School of Economics. During his doctoral research, he lived with the Barolong boo Ratshidi tribe on the border between South Africa and Botswana. While researching in the tribal capital, he discovered Plaatje's diary.

Dr Comaroff is currently a lecturer in social anthropology at the University of Manchester. He is presently preparing further work on the Bantu-speaking peoples of South Africa.

# THE BOER WAR DIARY
# OF SOL T. PLAATJE

An African at Mafeking

edited by
John L. Comaroff

# CONTENTS

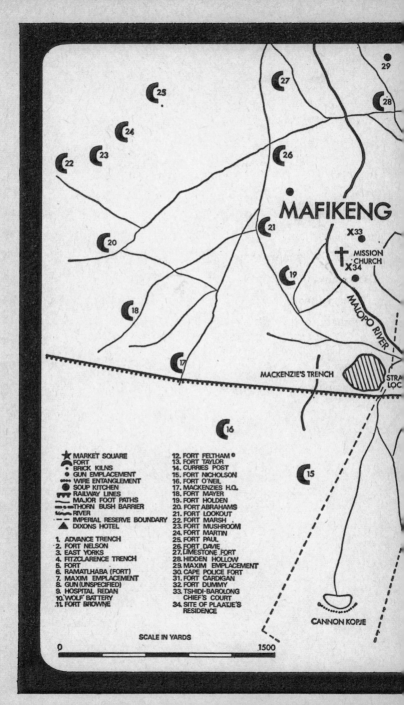

MAFIKENG

X33

† MISSION
CHURCH
X34

MALOPO RIVER

MACKENZIE'S TRENCH

STRA
LOC

★ MARKET SQUARE
☾ FORT
● BRICK KILNS
● GUN EMPLACEMENT
✕ WIRE ENTANGLEMENT
⚒ SOUP KITCHEN
⊞ RAILWAY LINES
⋯ MAJOR FOOT PATHS
▬▬ THORN BUSH BARRIER
〰 RIVER
– – IMPERIAL RESERVE BOUNDARY
▲ DIXONS HOTEL

1. ADVANCE TRENCH
2. FORT NELSON
3. EAST YORKS
4. FITZCLARENCE TRENCH
5. FORT
6. RAMATLHABA (FORT)
7. MAXIM EMPLACEMENT
8. GUN (UNSPECIFIED)
9. HOSPITAL REDAN
10. WOLF BATTERY
11. FORT BROWNE

12. FORT FELTHAM ●
13. FORT TAYLOR
14. CURRIES POST
15. FORT NICHOLSON
16. FORT O'NEIL
17. MACKENZIES H.Q.
18. FORT MAYER
19. FORT HOLDEN
20. FORT ABRAHAMS
21. FORT LOOKOUT
22. FORT MARSH
23. FORT MUSHROOM
24. FORT MARTIN
25. FORT PAUL
26. FORT DAVIE
27. LIMESTONE FORT
28. HIDDEN HOLLOW
29. MAXIM EMPLACEMENT
30. CAPE POLICE FORT
31. FORT CARDIGAN
32. FORT DUMMY
33. TSHIDI-BAROLONG
    CHIEF'S COURT
34. SITE OF PLAATJE'S
    RESIDENCE

CANNON KOPJE

SCALE IN YARDS

0                                    1500

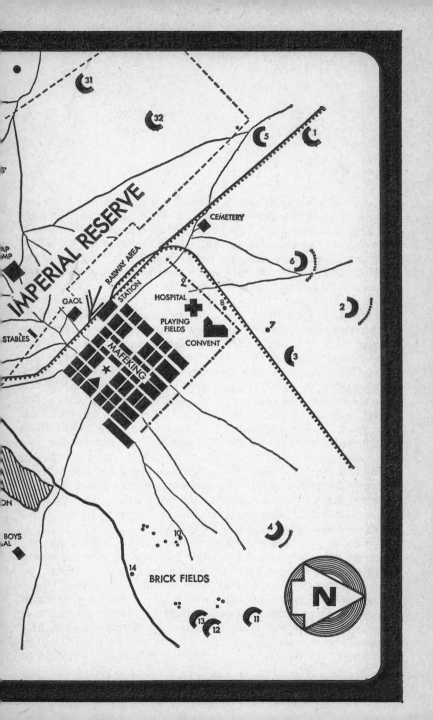

# PREFACE

The diary of Solomon Tshekisho Plaatje [1] is indisputably an important piece of Africana. It is significant, apart from all else, in that it records the siege of Mafeking from a hitherto neglected vantage-point. For, in the polyglot community that constituted this theatre of the Anglo-Boer War, the largest component was neither British nor Boer. It was the Barolong boo Ratshidi, the tribe which established what was, perhaps, the most famed outpost of the British Empire at the turn of the century. Yet, in the hue and cry that followed the relief of Mafeking, little serious attention was paid to the role of these tribesmen. It is true that in the celebrations after the relief they were not totally excluded; representatives of both the military and the civilian authorities participated in congratulatory meetings in their village. But, in the literature that immortalised the defence of the remote border settlement, the Barolong are generally discussed in a rather desultory manner. For the first time the events of the siege are recounted from their point of view. This aspect of Plaatje's contribution is certainly significant; but, even more than presenting a novel view of a fascinating period in South African (and indeed British) history, the diary affords insight into the character of its author as a young man. In the light of the fact that Plaatje was, in the first three decades of this century, to play a key role in South African political history, this is certainly important. The diary of Sol T. Plaatje is not merely a record of the siege of Mafeking. It is a portrait of the development of a young African intellectual in an era during which the future of his people was being moulded.

The document was discovered by accident rather than by design. The Barolong among whom Plaatje lived during the siege were unaware of its existence. It came to light through an unexpectedly fortunate incident. During the course of a period of anthropological fieldwork among the Barolong boo Ratshidi, I let it be known that I was interested to see any old letters or documents that the tribesmen might have accumulated. There was no available mass medium to publicise this request, other than the informal communication network in the village. As is usual, however, the news spread rapidly. Barolong, who have an insatiable interest in any written record of their own history, responded enthusiastically, and numerous items of diverse content and condition found their way into my possession. A young friend whom I had forgotten to ask heard of my search by chance. He is a direct descendant of the founder of Mafeking and a grandson of Sol Plaatje. Unsolicited, he proffered a tatty leather scrapbook and explained that it had once belonged to his grandfather.

Long after the siege Plaatje's daughter, Violet, married Morara Molema, a member of the Barolong boo Ratshidi nobility and a son of the man with whom the diarist had lived during his sojourn in Mafeking. Before his death in 1932, Plaatje, who had by then become an established author and polemicist, gave the scrapbook to Violet apparently with little explanation of its content. He had left Mafeking and its memories far behind. The old diary, which must have appeared naïve and clumsy to the now experienced writer, was ignored. Violet Molema passed the book on to her son, Victor. Since last being used it had lain unopened under a pile of books and other memorabilia. When he heard that old documents were being sought, its owner extricated it from the literary rubbish-dump.

The scrapbook itself contained little of interest. Occasional pages were covered in scrawled notes on a variety of personal matters; but there was little else. It was only when some sheets of foolscap slid from under its back cover that the scrapbook yielded its bounty. Over the years the weight that lay on top of it had moulded it into a protective sheath for the foolscap sheets. Unprotected, the diary probably would not have survived in an environment where rodents and abrasive dust destroy all but the most carefully hidden documents. The pages on which the entries were written showed evidence of once having been bound as a notebook; remnants of blue cloth still adhered to them. The paper was brittle and yellowed with age, but the script – including, remarkably, even the sections in pencil – was almost entirely legible.

The diary of Sol T. Plaatje was discovered almost seventy years after the date of the first entry. Ironically, perhaps, its discovery occurred during the year in which the assembly of the Tswana Territorial Authority (colloquially, the Tswana *bantustan* government) met for the first time at its official new capital – Mafeking. In 1899 Boer and Briton fought a white man's war to decide, among other things, the future of black South Africa. The confrontation to which Plaatje was a witness occurred on African soil, yet the participation of Barolong (who may be seen to have instigated the British presence in the area in the first place) was limited by the dictates of two external parties. Today there are in Mafeking descendants of both Boer and British participants; they still live alongside the Baronlong. The former adversaries are no longer separated by a line of investment. A new boundary, however, divides the Mafeking district. For Barolong territory now falls into a series of Bantu reserves that are collectively a part of the Tswana *bantustan*. The régime has changed, but, in the broadest sense, the position of the Barolong has not. Plaatje was implacably opposed to the policy of the establishment of 'native reserves' and the assumptions that lay behind it. He later wrote, as his first published work, an eloquent polemic against the Natives' Land Act of 1913 in which this policy was embodied. The siege, as a war epic, is all but forgotten. But the history of Mafeking represents, in a microcosm, the broader issue of the development of inter-community relations in South Africa.

As will become evident, the editing of this manuscript required a multi-faceted series of skills, to most of which the editor can lay little claim. As a result, many debts of gratitude were incurred. Perhaps the first was to Victor Molema, the owner of the diary. Apart from making the manuscript available for editing, he offered his unstinting co-operation whenever it was needed. Other Barolong friends also contributed in no small measure. Many gave up hours of their time in patient discussion of Plaatje's linguistic usage; others volunteered essential information, thereby rendering Plaatje's universe comprehensible. It is impossible to distinguish the debts incurred in the collection of the specialised data necessary for the editing of such a manuscript from those more general obligations that an anthropologist inevitably accumulates during a period in the field; the operation of gathering research material is not thus compartmentalised. Hence grateful acknowledgment must be made to Chief Kebalepile Montshiwa, his councillors and the tribe at large, who were our hosts and teachers while we lived amongst them.

I was fortunate in having the unfailing assistance of two outstanding secretaries for the translation of the occasional shorthand entries. Mrs Mairi Fraenkel and Miss Barbara Casper were faced with the unenviable task of deciphering a seventy-year-old, fading script. That these parts of the text have been made available to the reader is entirely due to their efforts.

Mrs Connie Minchin contributed to the preparation of the manuscript in a variety of ways. Apart from making available her siege-documents and maps, she gave generously of her wide knowledge of the relevant history, and of her time in checking the manuscript. Mr Joe Podbrey, currently editor of the *Mafeking Mail*, permitted me unlimited access to the siege-editions of the newspaper. He also acted as a source of encouragement and practical advice throughout; without his support the task at hand would have been far more onerous. He and many others in Mafeking provided unstinting hospitality and co-operation throughout the period during which the preparation of the manuscript – and the fieldwork project as a whole – were carried out.

Miss Beryl Podbrey, Mrs Winnie Bezuidenhout and Mrs Mairi Fraenkel undertook the typing of the numerous drafts of the manuscript. Mrs Rosalie Finlayson, who acted as a linguistic consultant, made constructive comments and suggestions. My wife, Jean, who at the time was engaged in her own research among the Barolong, was instrumental in preparing the diary for publication. An adept critic, her help was never withheld.

J.L.C.

*Swansea,*
*October 1971*

PREFACE NOTE
1 Pronounced 'plaai-kie'₂

# INTRODUCTION

One fine morning I became aware of a very smart, sprucely dressed young native standing to attention before me.

'Well?' said I.

'I hear you need a secretary-typist, sir,' he answered.

'Well, so I do. Is your master one?'

'I haven't a master,' said Plaatje, with a faint smile, 'but I write shorthand and can use the typewriter.' He spoke perfect English and I engaged him at a ridiculously low wage which he named himself and seemed glad enough to get . . . I recognised, in my new secretary, an extraordinarily capable assistant. To begin with, he could spell — which I can't and never could. He was quick on the machine . . . quick witted and understanding and quick to pick up and catch a new expression, ask the meaning and the derivation of it and add it to his vocabulary. As to what would now be called a liaison officer . . . he was invaluable.[1]

Thus wrote Vere Stent, the Reuter correspondent in Mafeking during the siege and later editor of the *Pretoria News*, of his first meeting with Sol Plaatje.[2] He could hardly have foreseen, in the spring of 1899, the future that lay before his new secretary or the influence this twenty-three-year-old Morolong was to have throughout black South Africa in the next thirty years; that he would become, in the words of an American publicity sheet, 'Native African Editor, Author, Missioner and Leader of his People'.

The history of Solomon Tshekisho Plaatje's ancestors contrasts sharply with the progress of his own career. His family traced its origins to Modiboa, who is believed by Barolong to have been their eighth chief. When he died his two sons, Mooki and Tshesebe, came into conflict over their claims to the chiefship. The latter succeeded, and the former, with a group of allies, hived off to form an independent splinter chiefdom. The descendants of Mooki called themselves *Barolong ba ga Modiboa* ('the Barolong of Modiboa') in order to assert their genealogical seniority. Seven generations later, after the Barolong nation had fragmented into a number of separate tribes,[3] one of the emergent chiefs endeavoured to reincorporate the secessionists by force. As a result the *ba ga Modiboa* were scattered and their component groups compelled to seek refuge within the various other Barolong chiefdoms. Today they still live scattered among the recognised Barolong tribes – and their lot is still one of political obscurity. Plaatje's ancestors had an early foretaste of political subordination; this was to follow for most of the tribes of southern Africa in the decades after contact with Europeans. But his own personal development represents a movement in the opposite direction: he rose from humble circumstances to a position of pre-eminence that transcended the narrow arena of tribal politics. If his political objectives were national, the strategic efforts he made to achieve them were at an international level.

Sol Plaatje spent much of his youth at Pniel, in the Orange Free State. There, as staunch Lutherans, his family were able to reside near the local mission station. Having been born, in 1877, near Boshof,[4] the move to Pniel was to prove significant for Plaatje; for, at the Lutheran Mission School and the nearby Church of England Mission, he received all the formal education he was to have. Under the instruction of the Reverend G. Westphal and the Reverend H. Crossthwaite, he took his first tentative steps in English and arithmetic and in the reading and writing of his mother tongue. Here he began to prepare himself for an intended career in the Cape Civil Service. But, although the mission station was the primary source of African education at this time, Pniel had limited facilities. As a result Plaatje could only continue his schooling until the completion of Standard Three, which is remarkable when one considers his later literary achievements.

An offer of a position as a postman in Kimberley removed Plaatje to an urban environment for the first time. There, it seems, he found an atmosphere conducive to self-education. Throughout his life the diarist was obsessed with the pursuit of knowledge; Stent's aforementioned observation underlines a typical piece of behaviour. By 1898, when he became the official interpreter at the Kimberley Magistrate's Court, he had taken the Cape Civil Service examination and topped the (multi-racial) list of successful candidates. Plaatje, as he proved repeatedly later, never chose willingly to do anything by the easiest method. On this occasion he wrote the examination in Dutch, the second non-Bantu language that he had learnt to the point of fluency in his twenty-two years. To add to his secretarial skills he then entered a typewriting examination and again topped the list of successful candidates. This performance was to be remembered many years afterwards in a situation that exemplified both Plaatje's role in white South Africa and the nature of the struggle that he later took upon himself. A Member of

13

Parliament for Pretoria, Mr Harm Oost, expressed concern at the fact that Plaatje had addressed the pupils of a white girls' school after tuition hours. In a reply written to a Cape Town newspaper, a correspondent wrote:

Sir, Mr Harm Oost . . . is concerned because Mr Sol Plaatje, a distinguished native journalist and author, addressed girls at a Cape Town school after school hours. It may interest him to know that years ago Mr Plaatje came here for a typewriting examination and topped the list of successful (European) candidates. The same thing happened when he wrote the Civil Service examination in Dutch. Does Mr Harm Oost see any harm in students listening to a native lecturer who outclassed their elders in the examination room 30 years ago? . . .

His transfer to Mafeking initiated an important phase in Plaatje's development. When he arrived, late in 1898, he was already an accomplished linguist and secretary; by the time he left, approximately a decade later, he had served his apprenticeship as an editor and public figure and was equipped to assume his role at the forefront of the emerging African national movement.

When he took up employment as interpreter at the Resident Magistrate's Court in Mafeking, the diarist was familiar with the three major groups that were to be involved in the siege. Always intensely conscious of his ethnic background, Plaatje seems also to have had an insatiable curiosity about his cultural roots. He had already been employed by the British Colonial administration for some months, and with the Boer community, he had had frequent contact, as a youth, in the hinterland of the Orange Free State. But the siege was to bring these three parties into direct confrontation, and Plaatje into the relationship with them that set the tone for his future political role. While employed in Mafeking he lived in the Tshidi-Barolong capital village with a family of the tribal nobility. With most of its male members having had a mission-school education and being active in church organisations, this group was both involved in Tshidi administrative affairs and concerned with African politics beyond ethnic boundaries. Plaatje's identification with the cause of African advancement no doubt received impetus from this close contact with the politically conscious Molema family. Indeed, after the siege it was Silas Telesho Molema who financed the first newspaper which Plaatje was to edit.

If his commitment to the African national cause took shape in Mafeking, so did his faith in the notion that it was to Great Britain that black South Africa should look for a political ally. This, as we shall see, was to be reflected in his later activities within the framework of the

South African Native National Congress (S.A.N.N.C.). During the siege his close contact with British authorities and British journalists convinced him that it was the Imperial government alone that was able to enforce a liberal 'native policy' as opposed to the more repressive approach of the Boer republics in the Transvaal and Orange Free State.

At the same time Plaatje's antipathy towards the Boer community increased, no doubt influenced by the fact that, living among the Tshidi-Barolong, he was exposed to virulent anti-Boer sentiment. The tribesmen and the Transvaal burghers were bitter enemies; half a century of land dispute had brought them, on more than one occasion, into open conflict. The fact that the young interpreter found himself on the opposite side to the republics in war could only have strengthened a hostility that already existed.

Mafeking was the stage upon which the political persona of Sol Plaatje began to emerge. During the siege the scope of his work broadened considerably. Although he remained the official interpreter to the Resident Magistrate throughout, the fact that martial law was declared immediately after the start of the war meant that he officiated in a Court of Summary Jurisdiction, over which Lord Edward Cecil presided. This, and the fact that Plaatje sold his secretarial services to the various correspondents who were in Mafeking covering the 'western front', put him in a position which gave special access to information. Some of this he committed to his private journal; but it seems likely that the experience itself provided knowledge and insight later to prove invaluable in his political career.

There was another aspect of his official responsibilities that was also to provide the basis for his future role. The Resident Magistrate, Mr C. G. H. Bell, was also Civil Commissioner, responsible for the administration of Africans within his area of jurisdiction. This duty continued through the siege, and Plaatje acted as his liaison officer. This took the diarist out of the relatively privileged circumstances of his immediate home environment among the noble and wealthier Barolong and gave him first-hand experience of the poverty to which ordinary Africans were reduced by the devastating rinderpest epidemic of 1896 and then by the siege itself. This, in turn, created in Plaatje an interest in the rural African populations that was repeatedly to become manifest in his later political struggles; unlike some of his compatriots, Plaatje was never to see the fight for African rights as based solely in urban South Africa.[5]

That Plaatje decided to keep a diary during the siege was probably unknown to most of his friends. No such document is mentioned by his biographers;[6] nor is it remembered by survivors who knew Plaatje at the turn of the century. It may not have occurred to him to keep a diary at first. This is a literary medium that has not proved popular among black South African writers, even in more recent times. It is possible that he followed the example set by the correspondents with whom he came into daily contact; several of them kept journals. That the entries begin approximately two weeks after the start of the siege would appear to substantiate this view.

Perhaps the decision to keep a diary was also influenced by the fact that this was a convenient way of exercising the novel phrases over which the author questioned Vere Stent and others so carefully. From the manner in which the journal was kept, its obvious tone of privacy, it is clear that Plaatje had no thoughts about ever publishing it. His first published work came much later, after he had had several years' experience as an editor, Lutheran lay preacher and secular public orator. But this earlier work constituted a vital link – tenuous though it may appear at first sight – in his progress towards international fame. During the latter part of the siege, Bell requested of his interpreter and assistant a weekly report on the 'native situation'. In the practised style that had emerged through his private journal entries, Plaatje wrote impressive communications. Vere Stent, who read some of these, tried to persuade him to leave the Civil Service for a career in journalism. Later Mr S. Cronwright-Schreiner [7] supported the Reuter correspondent, and together they prevailed upon him to do as they suggested. The world of African journalism was not, at that time, large. Plaatje, therefore, did not have many alternatives: he assumed the editorship of Silas Molema's Setswana–English weekly, *Koranta ea Batswana* ('The Newspaper of the Batswana').

Ultimately Mafeking was too small for Sol Plaatje. When, after seven years of publication, the newspaper closed down, he moved to Kimberley to edit *Tsala ea Batho* ('The People's Friend'), a trilingual weekly owned by a syndicate in Thaba 'Nchu, the Orange Free State capital of the Seleka-Barolong from which his mother came.

When, in 1912, the South African National Congress (forerunner of the African National Congress) was formed under the presidency of the Reverend J. L. Dube, Plaatje became its first General Corresponding Secretary. Through the medium of his newspaper and of the Lutheran pulpit, he had by now become a national figure. His opposition to the formation (in 1910) of the Union of South Africa was well-known: he had broadcast the fear of eventual Afrikaner supremacy and had predicted that legislation dispossessing Africans of basic human rights would follow soon after Britain relinquished effective control. Plaatje was not anti-white: his antipathy was directed towards the Afrikaner. It is true that he regretted some of the effects of overrule. Indeed, once when rebuked for ingratitude by a government representative and told to remember 'all the blessings the white man has bestowed upon you', Plaatje was provoked to reply: 'I do; I always do – especially brandy and syphilis.'[8] But it was against the repressive legislation – which he believed to be the result of Afrikaner notions of black inferiority – that he most earnestly fought. And his strategy – perhaps naïve in retrospect – was based on the idea that if Africans could prove themselves capable of 'adopting the ways of [western] civilisation'[9] white South Africa might be persuaded to respond by developing a multiracial ethos.

The Natives' Land Act, no. 27, of 1913, was the first enactment after the establishment of the union that posed a threat to African rights. A long and complicated piece of legislation, it provided, in essence, for the creation of 'scheduled native areas' in which Africans could own land. Outside these areas Africans were specifically barred from the future purchase or hire of land from anyone other than an African; within them Africans could not sell to non-Africans. Plaatje objected to the law on several grounds. In the first place it would leave vast numbers of black tenants on white-owned farms with a choice between eviction and servitude (which was permitted under the Act). Secondly, the scheduled areas were of grossly insufficient size; and, as they were generally held corporately by lineages, clans or tribes, the notion that individual Africans would be able to buy land was nonsense. This, in turn, carried a threat that Plaatje feared: it would encourage tribal consciousness and hence foster cleavage in an age when the African élite was encouraging the emergence of a national identity. But, most important of all, Plaatje foresaw this as a first step towards the dispossession of African rights; it represented the domination of repressive ex-republican ideas on 'native policy' over the Cape liberal tradition. Plaatje's perceptive analysis of events leading up to the passing of the Act does not obscure his central, cogently stated point: 'Awakening on Friday morning, June 20, 1913, the South African Native found himself, not actually a slave, but a pariah in the land of his birth'.[10]

Plaatje devoted his energy, his time and his modest resources to the fight against this legislation. Immediately after it became an Act of Parliament, he toured South Africa on a bicycle in order to investigate the effects of the implementation of the law. In his report (first presented orally at S.A.N.N.C. meetings and then published in *Native Life in South Africa*) Plaatje argued that the Act had angered and upset a considerable number of whites as well as the blacks, who were more immediately and drastically affected. It would seriously damage any hopes of mutual understanding and future *rapprochement*. Throughout he emphasised what he believed to be 'Dutch' inhumanity towards rural Africans, recording the plight of his people with a sense of dignity and pathos that makes this an eloquent and moving polemic:

During the same night [while on the tour] we were told of the visit of a Dutch farmer in the middle of June, 1913, to his native tenants. One of the Natives – named Kgabale – was rather old. His two sons are delving in the gold mines of Johannesburg . . . and return home each spring time to help the old man and their two young sisters to do the ploughing. The daughters tend the fields and Kgabale looks after the stock. By this means they have been enabled to lead a respectable life and to pay the landowner fifty per cent of the produce every year, besides the taxes levied by the Government on Natives. Three weeks before our visit, the farmer came to cancel Kgabale's verbal contract with him and to turn the family into unpaid servants in return for the privilege of squatting on his farm. As Kgabale was too old to work, the farmer demanded of him that his two sons should return immediately from Johannesburg to render manual service on his farm, failing which, the old man should forthwith betake himself from the place.

Naturally this decision came upon Kgabale and his daughters like a bolt from the blue. The poor old man wandered from place to place, trying to find someone – and it took him two days to do so – who could write, so as to dictate a letter to his two sons in Johannesburg . . . The week expired before he could get a reply . . . The landlord, in a very abusive mood, again demanded the instant arrival of his sons from Johannesburg, to commence work on the very next morning. Kgabale spent the whole night praying that at least one of his sons might come. By daybreak the next morning no answer had arrived, and the Dutchman came to set fire to the old man's houses, and ordered him then and there to quit the farm. It was a sad sight to see the feeble old man, his aged wife and his daughters driven in this way from a place which they had regarded as their home.[11]

Having been a member of the delegation that appealed unsuccessfully against the Act in Cape Town, Plaatje urged the S.A.N.N.C. to send representatives in an effort to persuade the Imperial Government to support their protest. But here, too, the African delegates, Plaatje again among them, met with stoic refusal; representatives of His Majesty's Government thought it undesirable to interfere in the internal affairs of South Africa. Reminders of African loyalty during the Anglo-Boer War, of former assurances of political protection, went unheeded. The outbreak of the First World War put an end to any hopes of success that the delegation might still have entertained. But Plaatje exploited to the utmost his period abroad: on every possible occasion he addressed public gatherings – usually under the auspices of religious organisations – in order to recruit public support. In addition he wrote and had published *Native Life in South Africa*. Both the book and the speeches created for Plaatje the image of being a spokesman for his black compatriots.

After a brief return to South Africa, Plaatje joined a second delegation to England and then travelled to the United States and Canada to 'render a lurid description of Native conditions in the Transvaal, Orange Free State and surrounding Provinces'.[12] But this time the journey ended unhappily: for reasons that have never been satisfactorily explained, the S.A.N.N.C., while financing the return fare of the other delegates, did not purchase a ticket for Plaatje; also, the Congress withdrew its promised support for his wife during his absence. As a result he was stranded overseas. The exact details of this period in Plaatje's life are not entirely clear; what is clear, however, is that while he was abroad he learnt of his daughter's death and soon after persuaded a shipping company to convey him to South Africa on the assurance that he would repay the debt within a stipulated period after arrival.

Despite these setbacks Sol Plaatje continued to devote his energies to the struggle for the protection of African rights, as before using the public platform, the African press and the Lutheran pulpit to do so.

Although the diarist had always retained a keen interest in both African welfare and education, it was primarily during the latter part of his life that he became directly and personally involved. Despite the fact that he faced financial embarrassment himself, he founded men's and women's welfare associations in Kimberley. According to a short biography written by his brother-in-law, I. Bud M'belle,[13] Plaatje decided that the only way in which effective African welfare action could be encouraged was through personal example. This he was always willing to give, and he spent some time travelling around central South Africa entertaining lepers in asylums with the aid of a fragile old cinema-projector and films. Furthermore, he took a close interest in the African temperance movement. All this voluntary work left Plaatje even more seriously impecunious; but Africans in Kimberley responded by collecting funds and purchasing a house for him.

It was to education that he gave most of his attention and, again, personal example was his prime strategy. In the firm belief that English literature should provide the model for young African writers, he began to translate Shakespeare into Setswana. But this, for Plaatje, represented only one aspect of a broader endeavour: for an African literary élite to emerge it was necessary for writers to produce works in other forms. His own first novel, *Mhudi*, was reviewed by the *Times Literary Supplement* (31 August 1933) posthumously. The critic concerned wrote that 'it is believed the only novel written by a South African native . . . [and] is written in English, which the author used with exceptional facility and understanding'. But Plaatje's most important contribution perhaps lay in the sphere of Setswana language. Already in 1916 he had produced a volume of Setswana proverbs and their translations, while during the previous year he had collaborated in the production of a Setswana phonetic reader. The eminent linguist with whom he co-operated on the latter project 'found him to possess unusual linguistic ability'.[14]

The composition of the congregation at Plaatje's funeral in 1932 bore testimony to his status as a public figure. South Africans of all ethnic groups – family and friends, representatives of church, government and press – heard eulogies of which Plaatje, an 'eloquent advocate of Native rights',[15] himself would have been proud. In the weeks that followed, newspapers in South Africa and the United Kingdom recalled, at great length, his many-sided achievements. For, despite his earlier dispute with the S.A.N.N.C. and the growing accusation that Plaatje had become too 'Europeanised' and hence less militant than of old, there seems to have been an awareness that his death robbed the African national movement of a respected negotiator, a powerful voice and a versatile littérateur. One obituary, written by a devoted friend, summarised the emotions that Plaatje seems to have evoked in his followers:

A great, intelligent leader; a forceful public speaker, sharp witted, quick of thought, critical; a leading Bantu writer, versatile, rich and prolific; a man who by force of character and sharpness of intellect rose to the front rank of leadership notwithstanding the fact that he never entered a secondary school. . . . Never have I found him autocratic, contumacious, or narrow of outlook. Whatever subject he touched upon . . . was treated with a brilliancy, humour, ability and finish that at once surprised and captivated, inspired and humbled me. . . .[16]

Those attuned to more dispassionate assessments of deceased statesmen will find this distastefully emotive. Yet it is not difficult to understand why Plaatje, as an energetic activist, inspired such extreme admiration. This was an era during which black South Africa still believed that the future of their country could be influenced, at least to some extent, by their own constitutional actions.

It is hardly necessary to labour the importance of the diary. The intriguing personality and historically significant career of Sol Plaatje are reasons enough to justify its receiving serious attention. Nevertheless, the document is bound to raise specialist questions for, among others, professional historians, linguists and *literati*; hence some explanation concerning editorial strategy is required.

To the historian the diary is of interest on several levels. As an account of the siege of Mafeking itself, the manuscript introduces some new substantive material. Above all it provides rich data on the *dramatis personae*, white and black, and alludes to characters whose names are absent from other records. Furthermore, the diary is written by a Morolong and is primarily an African view of the siege. The contribution of Plaatje's compatriots to the defence — as spies, providers of food, guerrillas and couriers — is recounted in detail and compensates for a serious lacuna in the existing literature. This applies equally to the question of the physical hardship suffered by tribesmen during the period of investment. Plaatje, perhaps more than anyone else, was in a position to present a full picture of the relations between Barolong and British under siege conditions. Thus, even more important than offering new information, the diarist presents a familiar situation in novel perspective.

By then already aware of the 'native problem' as a significant issue in the political future of the country over whose destiny the war was being fought, Plaatje did not hesitate to articulate his perception of the manner in which the siege related to this broader problem. As we have seen, the diarist lived among the Tshidi-Barolong nobility and was probably influenced both by their views on South African history and by their attitudes to the Boers. It seems reasonable, then, to suggest that Plaatje's attitude towards race relations reflect to some extent those of the Tshidi. If this is true, the diary provides an insight into one important current of African opinion at the turn of the century.[17] As already noted, it also constitutes a portrait of the *weltanschauung* of a young African intellectual who was to have a significant effect on urban African political organisation in the years after union. Plaatje was a member of a relatively new African élite that later attempted to foster concern over the black man's role in South Africa. The diary, although concerned with a specific military confrontation, provides one of the early statements of the conscious model of inter-community relations then emerging among this élite.

There is one aspect of the diary the relevance of which concerns both history and anthropology. This relates to sections of the text that refer to Tshidi-Barolong social organisation, demography and economy at the time of, and as affected by, the siege. Again here Plaatje does not address himself to lengthy or highly specific description. But some valuable data emerge. Thus, for example, the status of the chiefship and character of the chief receive attention — as does the question of relations between the tribal political authorities and the administration. Also, it is possible to extract from the text a picture of the manner in which age-regiments [18] were employed as units of para-military participation.

There is, inherent in this, an obvious problem of editorial strategy. Where a text contains as much unsystematised material as does this one, there is the temptation to use it as a basis for a full historical (and, to a lesser extent, anthropological) account, inspired by the novelty of perspective suggested by the author. However, this might detract seriously from the diary, which is indisputably more than just another history of the siege. Hence a different approach has been adopted. In order to contextualise the entries, a prologue, an epilogue, editorial notes [19] and detailed annotations have been added. This has been undertaken with the understanding that, for the historian, the diary should be considered as a source of 'raw' data rather than a definitive text.

To the student of literature the interest of the diary is two-fold. In terms of the development of a corpus of African literature, it must be one of the earliest works (and possibly the only diary) by a black South African. Perhaps it is the first in the English language. Plaatje, as we know, was to become a leading figure in the development of black South African literature, both in English and in the vernacular. The diary, unlike his later work, is not carefully edited by its author; it was not intended for publication and he has not attempted the literary perfection aspired to in *Native Life in South Africa, Mhudi* and his other published volumes. In this sense the personality of the author is displayed with far greater clarity here than in any of these later works. In the diary we see the humour and compassion, the determination and the faith that underlie his subsequent writing; but here it is not masked by any of the inhibitions contingent upon Plaatje's rigid perception of the rules of style, manifested so clearly later on.

The second aspect of literary significance relates to the actual use of language. Here again there arises an interdisciplinary interest – this time between literature and linguistics. Perhaps because he had no need for careful correction, Plaatje indulged freely in the use of words and phrases from Dutch, Sotho, Tswana, Xhosa and Zulu. But, as will become evident, this usage is not random. It tends to correspond, in the sociological sense, to the structure of the relationships and situations desscribed by the author. Thus, for instance, recounting the joyous Tshidi reaction to the sound of British Maxim machine-guns, Plaatje uses the vernacular derivation of 'Maxim', *makasono*, a word with far greater onomatopoeic quality than its English equivalent. The diarist, quite obviously, enjoys word-play; at times he indulges in it with childish exuberance. But the fresh humour that emerges should not obscure the insights implicit in his choice of non-English usage in various contexts. The clear sociological relevance cannot be mistaken – this mode of expression appears too frequently to be dismissed as a set of random or coincidental usages. Inherent in this is an important implication for the literary analyst: because the diary constitutes private, unedited composition, it represents a type of literary Rorschach test in a cross-cultural context, providing thereby an insight into an African's choice of English usage where this is not his mother tongue. Further, it reflects, to some degree, the manner in which southern Bantu expressive styles condition and influence writing in the English language.

The literary and linguistic significance of the diary raises further editing problems. In the first place, Bantu orthographies were far from standardised at the turn of the century. Thus many of Plaatje's vernacular terms are 'erroneously' rendered. However, it has been decided to reproduce these as written in the manuscript; linguistic experts will appreciate the factors determining the orthographic confusion and make the necessary corrections for themselves. With acknowledged lack of linguistic proficiency, the editor has provided translations for all foreign words, and, where appropriate, comments upon their usage have been added. These annotations, however, will be found by the professional linguist to be very rudimentary. It is certainly possible to write at length on Plaatje's use of language; but, as with the historical aspect, the diary is of wider relevance – and, again, the expert is invited to view it as a source rather than a completed text.

Secondly, there arose the inevitable problem of correction. The literary purist may well prefer to have had the diary reproduced as exactly as possible, without any alteration, addition or subtraction. But, bearing in mind that the text is of interest to several disciplines, a compromise approach has been adopted. Spelling has been corrected and, where essential, punctuation introduced. Under siege conditions Plaatje was often compelled to write hurriedly, and apparently lacked the time to correct his errors; but during periods of relative quiet these mistakes are usually altered in the relevant entry.

Changes of this order are, in terms of the substantive content, relatively minor. Also, where there is evidence of haste, of careless omission or of any other feature that can only be achieved from the manuscript itself, relevant annotations have been added.

At certain points in the text a second handwriting is evident. For reasons discussed later, it is deduced that this belonged to a second scribe whose abilities did not equal those of Plaatje. It appears that the latter dictated these passages, for the style is inimitably his own. But they contain frequent errors of omission, of spelling and of punctuation. Like the others, these have been corrected and noted.

On some occasions Plaatje introduced his entry with a full date; on others he noted only the day of the month. In rare instances he wrote elaborate inscriptions. Here again the text has been standardised. The same applies to certain inconsistencies in the spelling of names and places. Where, however, these were felt to be unimportant or, on the other hand, relevant to the context, they have not been altered.

Where words have been added to the text, they have been inserted in parentheses. Certain paragraphs were found to be lightly crossed out in the manuscript itself. Often these are essential to the context and, if so, have been included. In the case of multiple alterations the fullest possible version has been abstracted, and a footnote added to this effect. But, in all, the extent of alteration is negligible.

In the latter half of the diary, Plaatje wrote some entries in shorthand. There are three possible reasons for this: haste, secrecy or the desire to practise the recently learnt skill. Where there is evidence for any one of these possibilities, the passage has been footnoted accordingly. Shorthand is by nature imprecise and personal to its author. Hence it is possible to interpret the script within a (limited) range of probability. The final versions represent a faithful attempt to arrive at accurate and comprehensible translations.

Finally, the entries have been ordered into five chapters; each, except for the first, coincides with a calendar month. (In the first the few October entries are assimilated with those for November.) This has allowed for the addition, at convenient points, of editorial notes. These are intended to contextualise the entries in terms of the ongoing situation in beleaguered Mafeking.

A problematic feature of the diary is its incompleteness; the entries cease some weeks before Mafeking was relieved. The most obvious explanation is that it was, in fact, completed and the latter sections lost. But, for many reasons, this is unlikely. Plaatje began his notes on the first page of the journal. From then onwards pages were, without exception, consecutively filled until the last month of his entries. At this point his usually systematic style gives way to uncharacteristic omission and the leaving of blank pages. And then the entries cease. The remainder of the now unbound book, some twenty pages, is left totally unused. If Plaatje did continue his entries there is no reason to suppose that he would not have done so on the remaining sheets. Paper was, at the time, in short supply. The *Mafeking Mail*, for instance, was by then printing on any that could be found; spare ledger paper was extricated from its binding and used as newsprint. The luxury of a fresh notebook in which to continue his diary would not have been available to Plaatje, even if he had so desired. Furthermore, such wastefulness would have been out of character. All of the author's later notebooks are systematically inscribed. He never gives any impression of being impetuous or disorganised in his private work.

There are other, far more likely, reasons for the premature end of the diary. And, if they are valid, the author's silence speaks as powerfully as his words.

At first glance it would appear that the point at which Plaatje chose to stop writing was a most unlikely one. Although the situation in Mafeking was uncomfortable, it did not look nearly as bleak as it had in the previous month. A comparison of Chapters 4 and 5 will support this contention. The last entries do not speak of particular hardship. On the contrary, they are optimistic in their tone.

It is difficult to obtain clear information on Plaatje's activities or his disposition in the days immediately subsequent to the final entry. But informed guesswork is possible.

As it had done frequently before, the pressure of work now probably forced Plaatje to fall behind in his entries. He was, at that stage, playing an instrumental role in the organisation of the exodus of African refugees encouraged by the military and civilian authorities to alleviate the acute food-shortage. By the time that he had an opportunity to record back entries, the situation had probably changed for the worse. Although the final sections were written at a time when general morale was high, the period immediately after registered a significant increase in public pessimism. Rumours were spreading to the effect that Baden-Powell was purposely prolonging the siege and that he did not care much about the plight of the people. Whether or not these had any truth, the negative effect on morale was immediate – despite the Commanding Officer's strong denials. In the Barolong *stadt* [20] more and more people were succumbing to starvation. Furthermore, although it may appear trivial at first sight, Plaatje had, up to then, refused stubbornly to eat horse-flesh. A lover of horses, the thought of this was repugnant to him. For a long time he had managed to hold out, but at the time of the last entries he was probably being forced to make the distasteful adaptation. In addition, it is quite possible that Plaatje faced other setbacks. He had often been ill, and several of his friends had died. This was the continuing pattern. It is equally conceivable that the diarist, perhaps deeply affected by the general diminution of morale, realised that to continue reliving these events through his journal merely rubbed salt into an open wound. The diary was, in any case, an exercise in a foreign discipline. Its continuation might have demanded a degree of emotional effort that no longer yielded a sufficient return. In this light the text may be seen to represent an organic unity; it is, in this sense, complete.

## INTRODUCTION NOTES

1 Letter to the Johannesburg *Star*, 5 July 1932.

2 *Plaatje* is not an indigenous name; it is of Dutch origin. Adoption of foreign names was common at the time, but it has proved impossible to ascertain the circumstances in this case.

3 For the early history and ethnology of the Barolong, see Breutz, *Tribes of the Mafeking District*, 1956. Today there are several Barolong tribes. The four main branches of the former nation are named after their eponymous founders: Barolong boo Ratlou, Barolong boo Ratshidi, Barolong boo Rapulana and Barolong boo Seleka. (These, again, are subdivided into the various Barolong tribes.) The two tribes that feature prominently in the text are the second and third; they were allied with Britain and the Boers respectively. In the notes they are referred to by the accepted foreshortenings, Tshidi-Barolong and Rapulana-Barolong (or simply, Tshidi and Rapulana). The fragmentation of the nation occurred in *c.* 1780.

4 Also in the Orange Free State, his small town is less than thirty miles from Kimberley.

5 Cf. Plaatje, *Native Life in South Africa*, n.d.

6 After his death there appeared, both in the South African Press and in pamphlet form, several short biographies of Plaatje.

7 He was the husband of Olive Schreiner, the South African authoress.

8 Letter from Vere Stent to the Johannesburg *Star*, 31 Aug. 1932.

9 This is a phrase that Plaatje himself uses in the diary when satirising a character whom he and a friend discussed for their amusement.

10 Plaatje, *Native Life in South Africa*, p. 17.

11 *Ibid.*, pp. 78–9.

12 This quotation is extracted from a publicity sheet circulated prior to Plaatje's appearance in Chicago, U.S.A.

13 This unpublished version (it appears that he wrote several) was found among the notes of Dr S. M. Molema and kindly made available to me by his widow, Mrs L. Molema.

14 The linguist concerned was Professor Daniel Jones (University College, London). It is quoted by C. M. Doke, a South African linguist, in an obituary, (*Umteteli wa Bantu*, 25 June 1932).

15 London *Times*, obituary notice (28 July 1932).

16 H. E. Dlhomo, 'An Appreciation', (*Umteteli wa Bantu*, 25 June 1932).

17 It should be remembered in this regard that the Tshidi-Barolong had played an active role in regard to nineteenth-century Boer aspirations, and had displayed a willingness to continue to fight for British control of southern Africa. See Molema, *Montshiwa*, 1966; Matthews, 'A Short History of the Tshidi-Barolong', 1945.

18 The Tswana tribes, of whom the Tshidi-Barolong are one, had a traditional system by which men and women were, after their initiation, recruited to age-regiments which were formed every four to seven years. The male regiments formerly constituted the units of a tribal army. See Schapera, *The Tswana*, 1953.

19 These are notes, added at the end of each chapter, which are intended to present some background material against which Plaatje's entries may be more meaningfully understood.

20 Dutch; 'town'. This word was, and still is, used by both the Barolong and whites in Mafeking to describe the tribal capital; it derives from nineteenth-century Boer usage.

# PROLOGUE

The story of Mafeking begins early in the nineteenth century, long before the establishment of the town itself. Before white farmers had begun to leave the coast and move deeper into the South African heartland, a series of tribal wars had set the indigenous African population in motion. The chain-reaction of belligerent campaigns reached into the furthest corners of southern Africa. The Barolong nation, which had, before the turn of the eighteenth century, fragmented into its several component tribes, found itself in the midst of the resultant confusion as it was attacked by the Matabele of Mzilikazi and the Batlokwa of Mma-Nthatisi in turn. The Barolong boo Ratshidi, who were then living in the Molopo district, on what is now the South Africa-Botswana border, took refuge alongside the remaining Barolong tribes at Thaba 'Nchu, approximately 230 miles south-east of their former homeland.

The Tshidi spent seven years at this refuge – between 1834 and 1841. During this period a Voortrekker party under Andries Hendrik Potgieter visited the Barolong stronghold. On their arrival they did not spend more than a few days with the Barolong. But a few months after they had settled on a piece of land given to them by a near-by Bataung chief they were attacked and dispossessed of their cattle by Mzilikazi's regiments. Potgieter sent his brother to the Barolong chiefs who, after hearing of the Boer plight, sent them cattle. The alliance thus established was mutually exploited when the two parties later combined to defeat Mzilikazi and put him to flight. It seems that the chiefs were under the impression that, in return for their participation, the Voortrekkers would acknowledge their right to occupy their former territories, despite Potgieter's rather grandiose claim to the possession – by right of conquest – of much of central South Africa north of Orange River. Boer and Barolong obviously had very different views of the implications of their former alliance.

When, after a long series of migrations, the Barolong boo Ratshidi returned to the Molopo in 1848, they assumed that their territorial rights would not be questioned. But the Boer leaders had not intended this at all, and a lengthy series of disputes ended the alliance and mutual goodwill. When the young Tshidi chief, Montshiwa, refused to acknowledge his servitude to the newly independent Boer republic north of the Vaal river, he was instructed – in terms of an agreement of subordination allegedly entered into with representatives of the Transvaal – to join battle against the Bakwena further north. He refused and, in 1852, before the threatened 'punishment' could be fully effected by the local Boer commander, fled with most of the tribe to Moshaneng in Bangwaketse country. But this refuge, some sixty-five miles north-west of Mafeking, was remote and imposed limits on Montshiwa's strategic control of the Molopo region. Realising that occupation is nine-tenths of possession, the exiled chief dispatched five of his brothers, each with a small following, to create a ring of settlements aimed at forestalling the westward expansion of the Boers. One brother was sent to establish a village along the Molopo river. He chose a site in the centre of the claimed tribal territory and named it the Place of Rocks, *Mafikeng*, in recognition of its predominant topographical feature. This brother, Molema, was the leader of the small Christian sector of the tribe and his dispatch also removed a potential internal threat to tribal unity. Molema and his small band reached their destination early in 1857.[1]

The sites chosen for the ring of settlements were selected primarily for their defensibility, and this proved a wise decision from the point of view of the tribesmen. For, however strongly Montshiwa complained of Boer encroachment on his traditional lands, the Boers were equally vociferous in claiming that the Tshidi-Barolong had no right to retain this land at all. It is unnecessary to follow the three decades of turgid debate over the matter. Later, when verbal aggression led to the outbreak of hostilities, Chief Montshiwa himself moved to Mafikeng and – at the insistence of Molema – established the tribal capital there. The little village became the centre of the Tshidi universe; and, as it did so, it assumed symbolic importance for the Boers who resented the chief and his attempts to persuade the Imperial government to aid him in thwarting the expansion of the Transvaal. Thus Mafeking represented the British thorn in the side of Boer aspirations. And Montshiwa was bitterly resented for his part in this.

Matters came to a head in 1881 when a junior Barolong tribe, the Rapulana, who had been attacked by the Tshidi and driven off their land, recruited aid from a third Barolong tribe and a group of European freebooters and drove Montshiwa out of one of his strongholds, Dithakong. The peace concluded after this dispossessed the chief of a considerable portion of land, some of which was given to the European allies of the Rapulana, who founded the Republic of Goshen. But the cessation of hostilities did not last long, and the Goshenites and Montshiwa were soon at war. On the advice of Cecil Rhodes, who at this stage was resident on behalf of the British Government in Bechuana-land, Sir Charles Warren was sent in 1885 with a force to 'restore order . . . and to defend the Native tribes who had placed themselves under British protection'.[2]

Under the name British Bechuanaland, the Imperial government annexed the territory 'north of the Cape Colony, south of the Ramatlha-bama Spruit and Molopo river, west of the South African Republic'.[3] It was then that Sir Sidney Shippard, who was appointed Administrator, Chief Magistrate and Supreme Chief of the Natives of British Bechuana-land, created the European settlement of Mafeking about a mile from Montshiwa's court. Thus there are two towns of Mafeking: Barolong *Mafikeng*, and the later-established European settlement, the name of which is a corruption of the original.[4] Their co-existence, and the events which led to it, explain – at least in some measure – why the border town was besieged. It is true that, from the Boer point of view, Mafeking was a convenient point from which to commence their offensive on the western front when the South African War broke out on 11 October 1899. But its ultimate strategic importance is questionable – so much so that this has caused speculation to the effect that the Boers made a grave error in committing a large force to a 217-day siege that, even if it had been successful, would have yielded small long-term military return. For the Boers could have by-passed the town and deployed their troops elsewhere. But, for them as for the British and the Barolong, Mafeking represented the confluence of competing interests in South Africa at the time; its significance was more than merely strategic.

In the fourteen years since the establishment of Mafeking (as opposed to *Mafikeng*) a community of about 1,500 had developed – a neat little railway centre of divers population. By then transferred to the Cape Colony,[5] the town had been built around a spacious market-square with the town offices in the middle. The new Victoria Hospital and convent constituted its northernmost buildings. Apart from railway installa-tions, the town could boast many communal facilities: a race-course and a recreation ground, a courthouse and gaol, schools, churches, a masonic hall, hotels, a bank, a library and several shops.

In anticipation of the war, Colonel R. S. S. Baden-Powell had arrived in southern Africa in July 1899. His orders were to raise two battalions and train them, and to take charge of the Rhodesian and Bechuanaland Police. But, above all, he was warned to be discreet about his activities for fear of antagonising not only the enemy, but also those allies who were afraid that any military preparation might be construed as an act of aggression. Most of the training took place at Ramatlhabama, across the Bechuanaland Protectorate border. Here, too, Baden-Powell, as officer commanding the North-Western Forces, decided to split his strength and to dispatch a regiment (under Colonel Plumer) to Tuli on the Limpopo river; the defence of Rhodesia was also his responsibility. Until September permission for the newly trained corps to move into Mafeking was withheld; but eventually the Cape authorities relented and allowed an armed force to be placed in town to guard the stores that had arrived by rail. Baden-Powell promptly transferred the entire garrison, for the order had not specified any number of men. Even in Mafeking their activities were kept secret from the townspeople, though the authorities (the Mayor, Resident Commissioner and Resident Magistrate) were drawn into the secret preparations. Above all, they feared the presence of Boer spies in the town, for the population included several families of Dutch descent.

By the time that the siege was laid, the defenders of Mafeking had been divided into several contingents. The Mayor, Mr H. Whiteley, officially called for men to form a Town Guard, and about 300 enrolled. A group of half-breed coloureds formed the sixty-strong corps of 'Cape Boys', while the Black Watch was composed of volunteers who, being non-Barolong, lived in the 'strangers' location' outside the town. One hundred railway employees organised themselves into the 'Railway Volunteers'. The Tshidi, while not forming a separate contingent, provided a number of volunteers who were variously deployed during the siege. These civilians manned the inner defences of the town, and served as a labour force.

The militia itself was composed of four detachments: the Protectorate Regiment (21 officers and 448 men), the Bechuanaland Rifles (5 officers and 77 men), the British South African Police (10 officers and 81 men) and the Cape Police (4 officers and 99 men). This garrison of 745 soldiers was mounted and armed with Lee-Metford rifles and, when they ran short, obsolete Martini-Henrys. Artillery support was bound to be scanty, for apart from four outdated seven-pounders (all muzzle-loading) the total armoury comprised a one-pounder Hotchkiss, a three-quarter-pounder Nordenfeld, seven Maxim ·303 machine-guns and two small quick-firers.

The defence installations were no less crude. Although small forts were being built and linked to Baden-Powell's headquarters at Dixon's Hotel by field telephone, it was a long time before an effective network of barricades and protective structures established Mafeking as a tightly knit stronghold.

This bleak situation at the start of the siege was ameliorated by the recruitment of an armoured train. Equipped with arms and ammunition, this provided a highly mobile and effective weapon. Stores of dynamite were also to prove useful in a number of defensive situations. But all this added up to very little when contrasted with the reports of Boer strength. It is almost impossible to assess accurately the size of the be-sieging force. Organised into 'Commandos' which were recruited by district, the number of men engaged at Mafeking fluctuated during the siege. However, there were times when the Boers outnumbered the British by eleven to one. A tough and determined body of men, they were mounted and carried Mauser rifles which had been well supplied with ammunition. Their artillery comprised at least ten modern pieces of various sizes, apart from the ninety-four-pounder that arrived in Mafeking towards the end of October.

Baden-Powell, after reviewing the situation, became convinced that it was advisable to include the Tshidi-Barolong *stadt* in the invested area if the Boers besieged the town. The morality of this has been questioned, but from a military point of view it was doubtless a wise thing to do. According to Plaatje,[6] the Tshidi-Barolong were quite ex-plicit about the desire to participate in the defence:

The Barolong and other native tribes near Mafeking were keenly interested in the negotiations that preceded the Boer War. The chiefs continually received information regarding the mobilisation of the Boer forces across the border. This was conveyed to the Magistrate of Mafeking with requests for arms for the purpose of defence. The Magistrate replied each time with confident assurance that the Boers would never cross the boundary into British territory. The Transvaal boundary is only ten or twelve miles from the magistracy. The assur-ances of the Magistrate made the Natives rather restive; the result was that a deputation of Barolong chiefs had a dramatic interview with the Magistrate, at which the writer acted as interpreter. The chiefs told the Magistrate that they feared he knew very little about war if he thought that belligerents would respect one another's boundaries. He replied in true South African style, that it was a white man's war, and that if the enemy came, His Majesty's white troops would do all the fighting and protect the territories of the chiefs. We remember how chief Montshiwa and his councillor Joshua Molema went round the Magistrate's chair and crouching behind him said: 'Let us say, for the sake of argument, that your assurances are genuine, and that when trouble begins we hide behind your back like this, and, rifle in hand, you do all the fighting because you are white; let us say, further, that some Dutchmen appear on the scene and they outnumber and shoot you: what would be our course of action then? Are we to run home, put on skirts and hoist the white flag?'

Chief Motshegare pulled off his coat, undid his shirt front and baring his shoulder and showing an old bullet scar, received in the Boer-Barolong war prior to the British occupation of Bechuanaland, he said: 'Until you can satisfy me that His Majesty's white troops are impervious to bullets, I am going to defend my own wife and children. I have got my rifle at home and all I want is ammunition.'

Baden-Powell, like the magistrate, stressed that this was to be a white-man's war.[7] He asked for Tshidi co-operation in so far as their village would be included within the perimeter of the invested town; but he claimed not to be keen that they take up arms. The inclusion of the Tshidi-Barolong did mean that a larger population had to be fed. But the commanding officer must certainly have known of Tshidi cattle-raiding ability; this could certainly have been anticipated as an important factor on the credit side. When it did later come to the worst, the fact that the tribesmen were rationed far more severely than the towns-people, and that death by starvation was rife amongst them did not alter his determination to continue holding out — or his rationalisation that the Tshidi-Barolong would have been much worse off in the hands of the Boers. Both Baden-Powell's critics and his supporters seem to agree that the Officer Commanding anticipated, and in fact desired, a siege. Both sides have used this to substantiate their assessments of his subsequent behaviour.

Thus the irrevocable decision to include the *stadt* was taken, and this certainly affected the nature of the siege. Oral tradition among the tribesmen has it that, although most of the Tshidi were in favour of supporting the former allies of Montshiwa, they were far from convinced of the military strength of the garrison. They remembered the British defeat of 1881 at the hands of the Boers. But, as the diary indicates, they turned out to be faithful allies.

This, then, was the scene in Mafeking at the outbreak of the war. Almost immediately after the commencement of hostilities Baden-Powell declared the suspension of civil law in favour of a martial régime and dispatched Colonel Hore and his Protectorate Regiment to a position on the eastern heights to await the Boers. Twenty-four hours were to elapse, however, before the first shots were to be fired — by the armoured train at a party of horsemen.

During the first week one serious battle was fought. But, for the most part, fighting was restricted to sniping and artillery bombardment. During this early period the terms of confrontation were tacitly laid down by Colonel Baden-Powell and General Cronje, the two commanding officers.

One cardinal rule was obeyed by both sides during the major part of the 217-day siege: there was to be no firing or any form of belligerent activity on Sundays. However bitter the battles of the week had been, the Holy Day was to be observed. Furthermore, there was to be no firing on the Red Cross flag flown on the mule-drawn ambulances that entered the scene of the battle once the soldiers had withdrawn. In addition, Baden-Powell requested Cronje not to direct fire at either the convent, occupied by the Irish Sisters of Mercy, or the Victoria Hospital. Later, when a camp was set aside outside the town (but within the lines of investment) to accommodate women and children in a spot safe from shelling, immunity was sought for this as well. From time to time the agreement broke down, and such instances were invariably followed by lengthy correspondence.

In these first days the attention of the garrison and the citizenry was devoted to improving the fortification within the six-mile perimeter of the besieged area. A minefield, which was three-quarters dummy and one-quarter dynamite, was laid to reduce as far as possible the number of front-line defenders required. The British South African Police (B.S.A.P.) Camp across the railway line from town and to the north of the *stadt*, was more strongly fortified. Thus the successful defence of Mafeking gradually became a more realistic possibility. That hostilities were restricted to relatively mild shelling facilitated this concerted preparation. But the situation changed radically on 24 October, for on that day the Creusot siege-gun began shelling from the Boer *laager* at Jackal Tree. The next day the besieged garrison had to repel an attack from the south-west, for the enemy believed that its artillery bombardment had significantly weakened the Mafeking defence. Another threatened Boer onslaught expected on the 26th never materialised; and on the following night Baden-Powell ordered a counter-attack on a strong fortification to the east of the town. In so doing he assumed some initiative in a not unduly optimistic situation. That the Boers planned another concerted effort was taken for granted. It was simply a matter of guessing the time and the place. This is the point at which Plaatje begins his entries.

PROLOGUE NOTES

1 This represents a highly simplified and foreshortened background to a long and complex historical process. For a more complete picture, see Molema, *The Bantu Past and Present*, 1921, and *Montshiwa*, 1966; Agar-Hamilton, *The Road to the North*, 1937; Mackenzie, *Austral Africa*, 1887; Matthews, 'A Short History of the Tshidi-Barolong'.

2 Matthews, 'A Short History of the Tshidi-Barolong,' p. 20.

3 *Loc. cit.*

4 Henceforth the European settlement is referred to as *Mafeking* and its Barolong counterpart as *Mafikeng*.

5 Annexation occurred in 1895, ten years after Britain established British Bechuanaland. (See Sillery, *The Bechuanaland Protectorate*, 1952.)

6 Plaatje, *Native Life in South Africa*, pp. 239–40.

7 Although by the end of the siege almost 500 Barolong had actually taken up arms, the role of the 'natives' was, as the diary indicates, a point of contention.

# 1 October–November 1899

*Sunday, 29th*

Divine Services. No thunder. Haikonna [1] terror; and I have therefore got ample opportunity to sit down and think before I jot down anything about my experiences of the past week. I have discovered nearly everything about war and find that artillery in war is of no use. The Boers seem to have started hostilities, the whole of their reliance leaning on the strength and number of their cannons – and they are now surely discovering their mistake. I do not think that they will have more pluck to do anything better than what they did on Wednesday [2] and we can therefore expect that they will either go away or settle round us until the Troops arrive. [3] To give a short account of what I found war to be, I can say: no music is as thrilling and as immensely captivating as to listen to the firing of the guns on your own side. It is like enjoying supernatural melodies in a paradise to hear one or two shots fired off the armoured train; but no words can suitably depict the fascination of the music produced by the action of a Maxim, which to Boer ears, I am sure, is an exasperation which not only disturbs the ear but also disorganises the free circulation of the listener's blood. At the city of Kanya [4] they have been entertained (I learn from one just arrived) with the melodious tones of big guns, sounding the 'Grand Jeu' of war, [5] like a gentle subterranean instrument, some thirty fathoms beneath their feet and not as remote as Mafeking; they have listened to it, I am told, with cheerful hearts, for they just mistook it for what it is not: undoubtedly the enrapturing charm of this delectable music will give place to a most irritating discord when they have discovered that, so far from it being the action of the modern Britisher's workmanship going for the Dutch, it is the 'boom' of the State Artillerist [6] giving us thunder and lighting with his guns.

I was roaming along the river [7] at 12 o'clock with David [8] yesterday when we were disgusted by the incessant sounds and clappering of Mausers to the north of the town: and all of a sudden four or five 'booms' from the armoured train quenched their metal. It was like a member of the Payne family silencing a boisterous crowd with the prelude of a selection she is going to give on the violin. When their beastly fire 'shut up' the Maxim began to play: it was like listening to the Kimberley R.C. choir with their organ, rendering one of their mellifluous carols on Christmas Eve; and its charm could justly be compared with that of the Jubilee Singers performing one of their many quaint and classical oratorios. But like everything desirable it ceased almost immediately. The Maxim is everybody's favourite here. Whenever there is an almost sickening rattle of Mausers you can hear them enquiring amongst themselves when 'makasono' is going to 'kgalema'.[9] Boers are fond of shooting. They do not wait until they see anything but let go at the rate of 100 rounds per minute at the least provocation. I am afraid if they could somehow or other lay their hands on a Maxim they would simply shake it until there is not a single round left to mourn the loss of the others. One can almost fancy that prior to their leaving the State [10] their weapons were imprecated by empyrean authority — and the following are my reasons for believing that the State ammunition has been cursed: when I passed the gaol yesterday afternoon Phil told me that while some prisoners were working in front of the gaol one of them was hit by a Mauser bullet (from the Boer lines) on the ribs. They expected the man to drop down dead, but the bullet dropped down (dead) instead. Immediately after, another hit a European's thigh. It penetrated the clothes but failed to pierce his skin; and just as if to verify this statement, another came round and struck the shoulder of a white man, who was shocked but stood as firm as though nothing had happened, when the bullet dropped down in front of him.

I have already mentioned that on Wednesday (the day of the all-round attack) I was surprised to find that on getting to town not one person was killed — while the Dutch ambulances were busy all the afternoon.

On Friday morning Teacher Samson [11] and 15 others crept along the river until they were very close to a party of Boers, who were busy sniping the location [12] from an ambush. They killed 8 of them and wounded several; they were all going to return without a hitch — but they advanced to disarm the dead men, and Samson received a slight wound on the shoulder.

Yesterday 22 Fingoes [13] went out to the Brickfields,[14] which may be said to be exactly on 'disputed territory': they took shelter among the bricks and killed several of them, which vexed the latter to such an extent that they fetched one of their 7-pounders and cocked it right into the kilns. Our men lay flat against the bricks, 7-pounder shells crashing amongst them with the liberty of the elements. They went for the bricks, knocked spots out of the ground they lay on, and shattered the woodworks of their rifles between and alongside them; in fact they wrecked everything except the flesh of human beings. It affused several of its mortal discharges over them and when convinced that every one of them was dead, [they] cleared [it] away leaving the 22 men quite sound, but so badly armed that if the Boers had the courage to come near they would have led them away by the hands. The gunsmith is very busy mending their rifles, two of which are quite irreparable, and the men are having holidays in consequence.

Our ears cannot stand anything like the bang of a door: The rat-tat of some stones nearby shakes one inwardly. All of these things have assumed the attitude of death-dealing instruments and they almost invariably resemble Mausers or Dutch cannons. We often hear the alarm [and] run outside to find nothing wrong; and such alarm was often the motion of the pillow if one was lying down. David was yesterday grumbling: 'Oh, what a restless life; if I knew that things were going to turn out this way I would never have left Aliwal North.'

After I left Mr Mahlelebe yesterday I came through the gaol yard onto the Railway Reserve's fence. Mauser bullets were just like hail on the main road to our village. I had just left the fence when one flew close to my cap with a 'ping' – giving me such a fright as caused me to sit down on the footpath. Someone behind me exclaimed that I was nearly killed and I looked round to see who my sympathiser was. When I did so another screeched through his legs with a 'whiz-z-z-z' and dropped between the two of us. I continued my journey in company with this man, during which I heard a screech and a tap behind my ear: it was a Mauser bullet and as there can be no question about a fellow's death when it enters his brain through the lobe, I knew at the moment that I had been transmitted from this temporary life on to eternity. I imagined I held a nickel bullet in my heart. That was merely the faculty of the soul recognising (in ordinary post-mortal dream) who occasioned its departure – for I was dead! Dead, to rise no more. A few seconds elapsed after which I found myself scanning the bullet between my finger and thumb, to realise that it was but a horsefly.

It is very difficult to remember the days of the week in times of war. When I returned from the river [15] early this morning I found David still in bed, and he asked me if there is any sign of their advance. He was dumbfounded when I said that they were not likely to advance as today was Sunday. What, Sunday? He thought it was Thursday (Ha! Ha!).

*Monday, 30th*

During this day we received another ultimatum [16] that if we did not surrender we would be bombarded early next day. We knew that the big gun had been with us for more than a week and as she failed to shake us in eight days I am afraid that the Boers are merely fooling themselves to imagine that we entertain any fear in being bombarded – for so far from being alarmed, we are getting used to it. I look back to reflect on the slight damage caused by these shells, nearly 200 of which have already been wasted on the town. Considering the expense of one of them (opinion on this point differs, some saying £35 and some £47), she [17] is really not worth the fuss. Meanwhile the position of the big commando at Lothlakane [18] is being moved down the river to a spot about three miles west of here, and one from the eastern to another spot three miles to the north.[19] We are anxiously waiting to see what tomorrow's day will bring forth.

### Tuesday, 31st

Long before 5 o'clock we were aroused by reports of Ben [20] going as rapidly as she did last week. She was accompanied by the enemy's 7-pounder and all other pounders. We woke, dressed in a hurry, and went to the rocks to find things really very serious at Makane.[21] They were shelling Makane and the dust was simply like a cloud around our little fort. The Boers were advancing towards the koppie like a swarm of voet-gangers [22]: they came creeping under cover of their shells, which were flying over their heads and preceding them like a lot of lifeless but terrific vanguards, until they opened fire with their muskets at long range. Their fire was very heavy, for the whole of the Dutch army had come over from all round Mafeking and turned their attention towards our little fort at Makane. They have evidently discovered that to capture the whole place at once was a hopeless task and they had therefore decided on capturing one by one of our forts until they have nipped every one of them in the bud.

As there was no chance of any bullets coming round my way I had a fair chance of admiring the whole of the proceedings. The Stadt had such an advantage over the situation that it was quite impregnable amongst the trees in the Molopo – while the surroundings are a wide, wide plain which one can examine from the rocks without being observed. That is one reason why Montsioa held out against the Boers for so many years.[23] He had only been defeated once, and that was when the tribe had their headquarters at Sehuba [24] before Mafeking was the capital.

To return to the subject. I think I have already stated that the Boers attributed their failure to the fact that we never leave our trenches to give them a chance of tackling us in the open: this morning they must have thought that they would easily compel us to do so by weakening Makane and naturally getting us to run to her assistance, thereby affording them an opportunity of going for us in the plain between this and there. If this was their expectation they were sorely disappointed, for nobody cared.[25] They went for the little fort from east, south and west with muskets and artillery, the former being volleys from about 800 hands. But nobody in town, or anywhere else, troubled his soul about it. The volunteers round the place, seeing that all of the guns were turned towards Makane, stood up and admired the operation as though it was a performance on a theatre stage. It must have given them a headache to find such a multitude of them advancing towards a fort occupied by 70 officers and men of the B.S.A. Police [26] – and nobody caring to go to their assistance. But this was not all: the enemy came quite close and still not a shot came from within the mysterious little fort. I believe the Boers (who always let off a number of rounds unnecessarily) must have thought that everyone was dead, for nearly 20 tons of bombs had already been plugged into the fort. The fortifications looked quite old and ragged in consequence. All of a sudden there came volley after volley from the dumb fort and we could see them fall when the Maxim began to play; some dead, some wounded and some presumably to wait until dark.[27] Their officers, who were mounted behind them and urging them on, were – with one exception – the first to run and at 9 o'clock they hoisted the Red Cross. Their ambulances and Natives were busy 'tutaing'[28] till about midday. Our losses were 2 officers and 5 men killed, and 6 wounded.[29]

This engagement was very unfortunate to me as it deprived me of one of my dearest friends in the place, in the person of the Hon. Captain Marsham. These experienced soldiers never care how fast bullets may whizz about them: they stroll about in a heavy volley far more recklessly than we walk through a shower of rain, and that is how he wrecked a career that was going to give him a name almost too heavy for his youth.[30]

The enemy having had the reverse of this morning's attack, we had a very quiet day.[31]

### Wednesday, 1st

Nothing happened during the day but in the evening my dear friend Mr E. G. Parslow was murdered by Lieut. Murchison – mentioned in the Official Publication yesterday.[32] This murder [33] has not only deprived me of a good friend but it has wrecked me financially. He paid for my little assistance [34] so liberally that I never felt the prices of foodstuffs that [have] reigned here since the commencement of the Siege. The cause of the murder is incomprehensible; but then reasons are hardly tangible.

### Thursday, 2nd

Nice and pleasant rains.[35]

*Friday, 3rd*

We have on this day received more shells than on any other occasion since the 25th. Ultimo. But we are gradually getting used to them and it is getting more like a holiday than a Siege.

*Saturday, 4th*

A shell burst near the church this morning and a fragment hit a Kgalagali's [36] arm, which was amputated – poor fellow. A Mauser bullet hit one Mrs Graham at the Women's Laager.[37] She was taken to the hospital where she is doing well.

*Sunday, 5th*

Guy Fawkes' day. The usual Prayers and Thanksgivings. Late last evening about 1,000 Boers were seen crossing from the southern Laars [38] over to the north of the town, but as it soon became dark we lost sight of them. Just about the time 'Au Sanna' always fires her 'bad-night'[39] shot we heard the report coming from the north instead of the south; we, however, thought little of it as it might have been that our ears were mistaken. This morning, however, it was discovered that it was a dynamite explosion that went off.

The railway line being on a gradient for a few miles north of the town, the Boers filled the trolley with dynamite, tied a fuse to it, lighted the fuse, and pushed it down the reclining line into town. Their intention was apparently to wait until the dynamite exploded somewhere about the railway station and killed everybody, when they would walk in and then publish to the civilized world that they had taken Mafeking at the barrel of the Mauser. But God forbade it and their determinations had been frustrated. The dynamite exploded a half mile beyond the graveyard, smashed the trolley that carried it, tore up the line and blew up the ground.[40] While some of us were paying homage to the All-Father in places of worship, some were busy arranging the line to prevent a re-occurrence. A very fine day. Soft and pleasant rains till eve.

*Monday, 6th*

'Au Sanna' gave us beans in the early morning and [at] about 8 o'clock she was moved from her old post to about two-and-a-half miles south-east of the town. They must have got a scent about the arrival of the Troops and are temporarily stationing her there, preparatory to her departure – if it is not for the purpose of getting a better command of the town. She gave her début at her new quarters at 3.30 in much the same humour and vigour as near Jackal Tree.[41]

20 Barolongs [42] under Paul [43] went to accompany 80 whites, who went to annoy the Burghers of the Laar down the river. More than 80

volunteered to go but on learning that they were not going to fetch the Dutch cannon which causes a great deal of annoyance from the west, all but the 20 got disgusted and declined to proceed on an errand with such a trifling design.

I find it easy to count Sanna's shots every day and will put every days's number in brackets after the date.

### Tuesday, 7th (15)

Early this morning we were woken by the rattling of muskets and artillery to the west, and specially pleasing was the 'bub-bub-bub-bub-bub' of the Maxim in accompaniment – and the whole affair bounced along and echoed away among the ridges in the distance in splendid harmony. The whole of the procedure was so entertaining that I felt I will not have cause to regret it when our men come back. Meanwhile we could see them heliographing half-way between the two Laagers and we know they were calling for reinforcements. Shortly after a force of about 600 mounted Boers could be seen circuiting around our range and making for the scene of operations. Our men got there in the dark and waited until they could see the tents very clearly, when they started peppering volley after volley in the middle of the camp, which was soon enveloped in a thick cloud of dust – and some Boers [were seen] running away half dressed. They continued to fire while they retreated slowly and the 20 of our people who accompanied the party said that everything was executed in grand style. They only regretted when they saw the Boers running away and leaving their big gun about 100 yards this side of the camp. They thought if there were enough of them they could have made straight for the gun and captured it, despite any European orders to the contrary. For it was only when the Boers saw that they were being reinforced that they came back to return the fire. All this caused the loss of 8 of our horses shot, one volunteer severely and 3 slightly wounded. Master Bell's [44] horse was among the killed. It was shot whilst he held it by the bridle. Later on we saw two ambulances busy. We spent a quiet day afterwards.

(Except that a shell burst in the hospital and considerably excited the patients. A letter was sent to Cronje,[45] remonstrating and telling him that.)[46]

### Wednesday, 8th (10)
### Thursday, 9th (10)

An occasional 'boom' from a piece of the State Artillery kept us in memory that we are beleaguered. Otherwise all week pleasant rains the order of the day.[47]

### Friday, 10th (8)

A Dutchman finished his term of imprisonment today. He was taken from gaol direct to Weil's Store,[48] where he saw, no doubt, that there was plenty of food in Mafeking. He was provided with his own choice in tinned food, biscuits and etc. – just as many as he could carry. He was blindfolded and sent across the line.

### Saturday, 11th

Today we had a shell at 6 a.m. and another at 10.30 and 'Au Sanna' never moved since. Oh, how we wished that she should be silent for good. We were only molested by the thinner artillery during the day, but those are not of much account.

### Sunday, 12th

We have a black Sherlock Holmes in the person of Manomphe's son, Freddy. He arrived from Kanya with some despatches this morning in company with Malno's brother-in-law: the latter was on horseback, which is very risky to cross the enemy lines with.[49] On Friday the horseman remained behind and Freddy came across a party of 60 Boers at Tlapeng.[50] He hid the letters and went straight up to them. They searched him for letters, and on finding nothing on his person, they became very friendly – more so when one of the party recognised him as an old good servant of his. They gave him a quantity of mutton which he roasted on the spot and had a fine repast at the same time as his Dutch friends. They left the place at 5 p.m. giving him an opportunity of fetching his letters. He reached his home (Ga-molimola)[51] in the evening and hid his letters in an ant-heap close by. Our friend the horseman, who met no Boers, arrived the same evening. Freddy advised him to return to the bush and hide his horse all day next day (yesterday) until dark, when they would plan the best way of getting into the town. Freddy became doubtful of the man's aptitude and requested him to hand over his letters to him for safekeeping, which he did. In the morning a party of 40 Boers rode past Modimola and asked Freddy where the cattle were. Subsequently another party (of 90 this time) also came past. After leaving Freddy's place, this last party observed the spoor of a horse. They traced it to a small village a little beyond. (Instead of going to where Freddy showed him, our foolish friend went to this village.) When the inhabitants perceived the party approaching along the horse's spoor, they decided to give them to understand that it belonged to the owner of the village,[52] and that his son had been riding it looking for stray goats. There was an interpreter of some sort who promptly advanced to meet the ephemeral conquerors of Mafeking and related to them the history of the horse. The head of the village – an old fool – overheard this, and blurted out that he was lying. This infuriated the Boers, who sentenced the interpreter to receive 55 cuts with a stirrup leather for his lies, and made a prisoner of our foolish friend while the interpreter was undergoing the sentence. When Malno's brother-in-law got arrested he whined and begged the Boers not to take him alone as he was not the only offender: there was another man, ahead with the Magistrate's letters, and they came from Kanya together. The Boers returned to Freddy who lied so classically, and with such thoroughness and serenity, that they disbelieved their prisoner's statement. They searched his person, his house, nay everything, but failed to find them; and Freddy walked calmly in here with both despatches this morning. From Freddy's information, the reason why we are having such quiet days is because the Boers have gone in different parties to loot our stock. We hope that by the beginning of next year they will be purging them back to us in much the same manner as they did 14 years ago.[53]

We spent this day in church. The pulpit was occupied by Mr Lefenya,[54] who warned his hearers to be very careful in their prayers, and remember that their God was the enemy's God; we, however, have the scale in our favour as we have never raised our little finger in molestation of the Transvaal Government, or committed an act that could justify their looting our cattle and shooting our children in the manner they are doing. The weather was fair and as shelling and Mausering were conspicuous with their silence, we wished that Sundays would come a little more often.

### Monday, 13th (2)

The enemy having gone to Kgoro, Phitshane etc.[55] to steal our cattle, we had a very quiet day. Only two shells came in from 'Sanna' and Mausers not quite a thousand.
(Shelling slow and Mausering mild.)[56]

### Tuesday, 14th (2)

Not a single shot during the forenoon. Lovely showers set in in the evening. And altogether one fairly concludes that life is really worth living, even during a siege.

### Wednesday, 15th (3)

Pleasant soft rains all day today. Some fighting in town without any results on our side. The cause of the abrupt decrease of our daily supply of 'Sanna' shells may be that they are running short of ammunition or that last Friday's Dutchman told them that the thing is doing us no damage meriting the expense and fuss they have in firing it. I have never had a shell burst near me, but this afternoon while I was at the Residence [57] one of them exploded somewhere to the east. A fragment came along, found its way through the roof, across the ceiling, hit the opposite wall and dropped on the floor. This was in one of the rooms, but I thought that the whole house was coming down on me and I could already picture to myself a number of volunteers picking up fragments of my body [and] piecing them together preparatory to them being laid in the grave. This, however, did not come to pass, for then I would not have been able to write any notes on the occurrence.

### Thursday, 16th

Heavy rains fell during the night, and they continued somewhat pleasantly all day today. This will soon [mean] a great improvement to the stock in the place as they are not permitted to go more than a mile for food. Besides, there are so many of them that the ground in the neighbourhood of the camp was quite naked. Bechuanaland grass, after a rain like this, takes a very short time to grow and by this day next week we will have the country as green as a garden. This, and the undoubted nearing arrival of the Troops, will render Rantho'akgale's [58] dream of starving us out an impossibility. A 7-pound shell from the east burst near the Railway Bridge: a piece of it came all the way from there and struck the pate of a piccaninny [59] in the Stadt. He bled very much but is expected to get through.

### Friday, 17th (17)

What a lovely morning after yesterday's rains. It is really evil to disturb a beautiful morning like this with the rattling of Mausers and whizzes and explosions of shells. 'Au Sanna' appears to have been sharpened up, for her fire was very vigorous and quick since 3 o'clock. Mausers were also very brisk today. Goodness knows what these Boers are shooting: they kill on the average only one goat, sheep or fowl after spending 5,000 rounds of Mauser ammunition – but very rarely a man. Thick clouds came up during the afternoon and by sunset we had very heavy rains. One of 'Sanna's' shells entered the sitting room at Riesle's new Mafeking Hotel and played havoc with the furniture. Mrs Graham, who was shot at the Women's Laager on Saturday the 4th, was in the hospital and progressing favourably: a fragment of a shell that burst near the Recreation Ground entered the hospital and frightened her so much that she broke one of her blood vessels and died in consequence. She was a young widow and leaves three little chickens to fight life's battle without parents. 'Sanna' was very sharp today, firing every 3 minutes instead of 8 as heretofore. She has either got fresh ammunition or a fresh gunner.

*Saturday, 18th* (4)

What a pleasant morning. One often wishes that it could be mutually agreed that both sides should lay aside their guns and go out picnicking, and not resume operations until Monday morning, January 1st, when the Troops will be in the country for certain. When I reached the rocks, I found the people arguing over the meaning of the unusual movements of the people in the Laager down at Koi-koi.[60] My field-glasses discovered that it was the enemy trekking, from one neighbourhood towards Lothlakane. Oh, how we wish them God-speed and a safe departure across the border. Everybody is so pleased at the Laager dispersing that very little attention is paid to Big Ben's outbursts. I went out for a ride for the first time since the Siege; enjoyed it so much that the sun set whilst I was still on horseback.

We have just got definite information that the Troops landed at Cape Town on the 4th Instant and that they are given 6 days rest prior to proceeding north. There is a general dismay in Fool's Paradise where their movements were not being studied before telegraphic communications were cut between this and the civilised world. Bets were freely entered that they would be here on the 30th Ultimo, then the Sunday after, etc., etc.; and bets are still pending that they will be here day after tomorrow. I have the honour of not sharing this dismay for, having expected them to reach here on the 20th, I prolonged my period to the middle of December when October went past and we had heard nothing of their whereabouts.

The prices of foodstuffs ran up to a very high degree: meat from 10d to 2/od per pound, bread from 1½d to 6d a loaf, and groceries and other necessaries in similar proportions. The office closed the stores on 12th Ultimo and did not even open to pay us at the end of the last month: the probabilities are that we will receive October's pay together with November's and December's at the end of the year, as relief appears to be as far as ever. The forage also rose from 4d to 1/6d per bundle but I was lucky enough to get free Government rations from the military authorities for our pony, who now feeds on Scotch hay and oats – and he is as fat as a slaughter-pig. He has, since the Siege, been working only with his teeth and I think it is his wish that Mafeking should be besieged a little more often: this, and the fact that I kept pace with the hard times by means of earnings from newspaper war correspondents [61] who (though not quite like my late lamented friend [62]) are fairly liberal, are good reasons why I should sing the twenty-third Psalm.

*Sunday, 19th*

I have forgotten to mention that some time ago the church bells, which were heretofore used for no other purpose than to remind the public that it was time to worship their Creator, have been turned to some other service; they ring in case of an alarm.[63]

The church bells, which have always been a comfort to Christians, are now a nuisance as they signify the advance of the enemy. During the first week of hostilities the alarm was sounded by a bugler, galloping from one end of the camp, blowing the bugle with all his force, while others echoed the strain to all corners of the camp. Since the arrival of this big thing [64] galloping is an impossibility and the church bells are substituted. One has to depend on this timepiece for Divine Service, which we very seldom attend as we do the whole week's work today. But in spite of all that the Humiliation, Prayers and Thanksgiving offered to the All-Father are of such far greater sincerity and deliberation than on an ordinary occasion.

It sounds much like a Sabbath morning when after 6 days of terror and shuddering (as though one had no right to live in this world) one has the liberty of breathing freely and enjoying the calm atmosphere, which gives the Sunday a more different and blessed aspect than the other days of the week. Saints and Sinners alike thank God for the leisure and wish that there were three Sundays in every week.

David trampled the back of a big snake with his booted foot last night. When the brute made for his leg he picked up a stick and killed it.

The Government have started a cheaper grain store for the benefit of the poor in the Stadt.

## Monday, 20th

Wireless telegraphs brought news that Cronje with his 3,000 men had been recalled, by orders from Pretoria, to reinforce the South.[65] He left the Marico Burghers under Malan and Botha to look after us. The big gun was broken, and another arrived on Friday from Pretoria, to relieve the broken one.[66] It is the intention of the remaining Boers to continue shelling until the inhabitants are reduced to eating horses (sick vanity), which they are sure to do as the Boers are able to stay around for a year or two. An American who carried Reuter's dispatches from here on Saturday last, slipped safely through the Boer lines.

'Au Sanna' was very brisk this morning, hardly giving us any time to dress and wash our faces.

Mrs Mahlelebe carried her 'drag' with great pleasure during these trying times and was yesterday delivered of a son – much to our relief. We can now commend both mother and son to the care of the All-Father with the hope that the heavy and menacing experiences of the past four weeks will not affect the life of the little one.

We are continually being cheered by news from the Natal Border. This is so interesting that we always forget our strain in congratulation of our forces there. How we would cheer if we heard similar reports from Kimberley. Altogether more shots were fired than on any day since the 25th Ultimo. 43 all told; this from the big gun only.

### Tuesday, 21st (6)

About 50 shots from the thinner artillery and 30 or 40 times that number of Mauser rounds in what we call a quiet day.[67]

### Wednesday, 22nd (8 × 2)

All of the smaller artillery except one 7-pounder, appeared to have left us and it is therefore easy to mention the total number of shots that visited us each day. The number 8 × 2 at the beginning of the first paragraph in each day's notes represents the number of shots fired by Sanna and the 7-pounder respectively.[68]

### Thursday, 23rd (10)

St Leger's [69] birthday. The weather fair and cloudy but occasional dust just prevents one from calling it a lovely morning.

Mr Molema [70] and I did our best to find a fattish sheep to slaughter in honour of the occasion but like everything in a siege we were only able to find one after a hot day's search.

The day was the hottest since the spring but soft rains refreshed us in the afternoon. We wished him joy and hoped that his next birthday would find him between both his mother and father and not in a similar state to this, when the distance and the enemy between (and with broken means of communication) completely debar one from sending him and his mother a congratulatory wire.

I was interpreting for the Officer's Board for the second time last night. I will be at it again this morning at 9.00 and tonight at 7.00.

One is always wondering whether or not a shell from 'Au Sanna' will not smash up the roof and crush our brains.

Such courts, however, transact a lot of business in a very short time as evidence is taken by a shorthand writer, which causes one to extremely enjoy interpreting, as you have to fire away without stoppages.

The Authorities have since the Siege been in the habit of 'gaoling' everyone (principally Dutchmen) suspected as a spy or of treasonable conduct. While there were a good many of them they planned the best scheme of how they could lock up the Gaol Guards, murder the balance, and clear out; like all lawless schemes this reached the ears of the Authorities and they were promptly brought to book. A Gaol Guard named Walker brought trouble upon himself by being associated with this party. The order says: William Walker, describing himself as a Scotchman, but preferring to express himself in Dutch, was charged with treason, but in the absence of an efficient and qualified Dutch interpreter, was remanded.[71] I have since joined the Court of Summary Jurisdiction.[72].

## Friday, 24th [73]
Hardly anything worth mentioning beyond the usual rattling of Mausers and boom of cannons.

## Saturday, 25th
The Summary Jurisdiction Courts are not as particular as our Divisional Courts, about punctuality. Night before last I was warned to be at the office at 7 p.m. I misunderstood the warning and went to the Courthouse until they sent for me half-an-hour later. Last night I was told to be at the office at 6.15. I misunderstood the time this time and turned up at 7.00. I thought that these warriors would pistol me as this was my second offence but they viewed the matter with total unconcernedness. This morning I turned up 10 minutes late. The shorthand writer was also fifteen minutes late. The Officers, finding me an irresolute, unreliable wobbler, engaged the services of a white man as the witnesses and prisoners were principally Boers – but the fellow being an amateur interpreter was completely flabbergasted when it came to cross-examinations, and I took his place to immense advantage. This lateness appears to be a disease with which I am infected and I will see it does not occur again as I feel very uncomfortable in consequence. This evening they gave me an opportunity of realising what it is to wait for others. We all turned up at 6.15 sharp but the Presiding Officer failed to put in an appearance. At 7.20 he was sent for and his excuse was that he had forgotten all about it. My patience was so exhausted that I would have knocked him down if I had the means. I was very restless in Court, for 'Sanna's' 'bad-night' shot always comes between 8.00 and 9.00 p.m. The Court was over at 8.55 p.m. When I left it flashed through my brain that 'Sanna's' close up [74] is always directed towards the town. I, however, had my doubts and wondered if this evening they may not prefer to knock spots out of the B.S.A. Camp. Then the whole plain I was to traverse would just lie in the course of the shell. I ran in order to cut quickly across this risky ground. I had no sooner reached the outskirts of the Stadt when a big red flame was visible to the east – and imagine my joy of the forethought, for around came the usual row, then the loud hum which turned to the side of the town and went to knock bits of brick out of the B.S.A. buildings. Thank God I ran and it didn't fly over my head.
(7 × 2).

*Sunday, 26th*

A lovely morning, no thunder; only prayers and thanksgivings. I sneaked the following from the Civil Commissioner's diary today:

> Boers came out of their trenches and sat in long rows on the embankment and gazed upon Mafeking with covetous eyes, and they no doubt marvel at our holding out so long after five weeks of continuous shelling. They cannot understand what became of us, as they never see anyone and the rat-tat of the Maxim and pop of the Lee-Metford are the only sounds emanating from this mysterious town.

Distant howls in the Dutch Reformed Church told that they held service there for the first time today. About 40 people went to the English Church: when there was much danger only 4 people went and now that there is practically no danger, 40 go. Surely the people of Mafeking are merely eye-servants of the Lord.

Malno left today for Kimberley. Gave him messages to Pniel and Kimberley.

*Monday, 27th*

Nothing worth mentioning. (13 × 11)

*Tuesday, 28th*

Last night a party of Barolongs were working at the Town Defence Works. 'Sanna's' 'bad-night' came round at 9 p.m. and burst just near them. Killed one, seriously wounded two and a fourth was but slightly wounded. If every one of these shots were to bag as much as this one there would surely not be a single fellow alive as the number spent on Mafeking is now between three and four hundred.

*Wednesday, 29th*

A fine morning. The hot summer sun in the east, with dark moving clouds in the west indicates rain. It is quite easy to walk in town today. The Dutch snipers being conspicuous with their silence, one walks with the privileged liberty of a fellow in Jones Street, Kimberley. Instead of the usual blood-stirring clapper of Mausers we are having that music so delightful to the ear when our guns are firing.

Captain FitzClarence was this day determined to give the Boers 'no show'. He went out to a little fort that has just been made beyond the Location, which places the big gun fairly within Musket range. At first he would allow them to load — then fire a volley at them. They (the Boer gunners) dispersed each time the gun was loaded and about to discharge a shot. He afterwards disallowed them even to come near her at all, firing at them every time they approached; practically making it bitter for them to approach their own gun. These things are not very beneficial to us as it is very hard to kill any of them. Still they are good as they show the Boers that they are not going to have things all their own way and this accounts for the nominal figure which represents our supply of today.

We had heavy rains since 6 p.m. It is still raining and is likely to continue all night and probably all day tomorrow.

Yesterday there came news for the *Mafeking Mail* that the Boers crossed the Orange River Bridge, Norvalspont, on the 5th Instant, and occupied Colesberg; that others crossed the Bethuli Bridge and destroyed the lines across the Orange. This is the line for Burghersdorp where my little family is and I can now simply commend them to the care of the All-Father; as Bud and the Judge President are most likely cut down below,[75] they will decidedly be in his care. All this is very puzzling. We had heard up to the end of October that Burghersdorp in particular was quite safe – but this was very embarrassing. This morning there came a dispatch (official) and threw a different complexion on the situation entirely: that the Boers attempted to cross the Orange River and found it impassable. One could almost fancy that yesterday's news was from across the border for it not only cast gloom on our side but also added that the Troops, who had done such splendid service a little while ago on the Natal side of the Transvaal Border, are now falling back to Estcourt and that the Colenso camp is smashed up in consequence (bad news). The whole of the country between the border and the Tugela is proclaimed Free State Territory. It now remains for us to judge whether we have to believe the *Mafeking Mail*'s service, or the Official Dispatch as the difference between the two is so great. I would, however, prefer to believe the Official service were it not accompanied by the following blood-stirring execrable lie: 'The big gun at Mafeking weighing ten tons, cannot be worked on account of heavy recoil.' Fancy sending trash to people who are under constant thunder from the gun that cannot be worked. The truthful – or truthfulness of both puts us exactly between the Devil and the deep blue sea – if it does not remove relief as remote as ever.

*Thursday, 30th*

Early this morning Captain FitzClarence was at it again and declined to give the Boers opportunity of coming near their own gun. This must have enraged them very much as they tried to approach in large numbers and knock the cheek out of our few naughty snipers. They were quickly silenced and we enjoyed that sweet and enchanting music from our musketeers. It gave us an entertainment of the sweetest music imaginable when slow volley after volley was directed at the angry Boers: now and then a 7-pounder would harmonise the proceedings with an occasional 'boom' in sweet bombardment, and the whole of the proceedings is as safe as at an Altar.

EDITORIAL NOTES

The diary entries comprising this chapter coincide with a distinctive period in the progress of the siege itself. Under General Cronje the Boer forces made a number of direct attacks on the town. The intention of the Boer commander was to bring about the defeat of Mafeking as quickly and as completely as possible. The advantage held by the Republican forces both in manpower and in arms made this a realistic possibility. The beleaguered garrison was quite aware of this, and Baden-Powell prepared his strategy accordingly. His comparatively small fighting-force could not afford defeat in the field, for they were hard put to man the perimeter of the besieged area. At the same time the Commanding Officer was aware that to allow his enemy complete initiative would have been disastrous both for reasons of morale and of logistics. Thus he planned quick thrusts at the Boer lines on the basis that, whatever happened, his forces should always have a line of retreat. It was a policy of harassment without involvement. That this succeeded is proved by the fact that morale in the town was high as sortie after sortie forced the Boers to retrench.

In the meantime defences in the town were being improved. A ring of forts (in telephone contact with Baden-Powell's headquarters at Dixon's Hotel) provided a constant watch on the perimeter, while trenches and redoubts sheltered the townspeople from the dangers of heavy shelling. Careful assessment of the food situation had proved encouraging, for nobody at this stage expected the siege to last 217 days. If it were possible to question the besieged citizenry about their hardships they would probably have suggested that – other than the sorrows contingent upon the deaths of close friends – lack of news and feelings of isolation were perhaps the most irritating of all.

A crucial event in the history of the siege was the departure of Cronje. With his replacement by Snyman the entire picture altered. Until the 18th the much respected General had caused the defenders many a headache, for he planned to vanquish Mafeking through direct attack. Snyman, on the other hand, adopted a far more passive – and pessimistic – approach. He relied on artillery bombardment – and time. Under him the Boer forces began the long wait; starvation appears to have been the fate which Snyman planned for his enemy. The wisdom of this approach seems questionable on purely strategic grounds – for this type of investment required a large number of men that might well have been deployed elsewhere; in a war on a territory as large as South Africa's mobility was crucial. Many have suggested that in adopting this position, Snyman did precisely what Baden-Powell had hoped for. This argument implies that the British military authorities wanted the siege to continue – at least until reinforcements arrived from England. For this would solve their problem of deployment in the face of a larger force, at least temporarily. Such extrapolations are easy to make in retrospect; they concern the broader issue of the allocation of forces across the country. The relevance for the people of Mafeking was more fundamental: it meant that, although they had to tolerate shelling, they could worry more about the problem of succour and somewhat less about the prospect of military defeat. True, it was necessary to be on constant guard; but the relative lull following Snyman's arrival allowed an opportunity for the organisation of the community, both civilian and military.

CHAPTER NOTES

1 Originally a Nguni term meaning (literally) 'not there'; now a popular South African colloquialism, it simply means 'no', when used thus. Its use in this context is interesting. Barolong, when speaking of a violent man, often describe him as being Zulu; in the traditional world-view, the Zulu are associated with military strength – a notion that derives from historical experience. Plaajte's use of a word that is commonly thought of in South Africa as being of Zulu origin, and its juxtaposition with 'terror', is obviously meant to be ironic. This is a day of peace – in a white-man's war. The thunder referred to immediately before is probably used here to mean shelling or artillery bombardment, though Barolong speaking English sometimes use 'thunder' metaphorically to mean 'death'.

2 On 25 October, General Cronje (then head of the Boer forces) launched a heavy attack. The ninety-four-pounder Creusot siege-gun – one of four bought from France – was set to work for the first time in earnest and was, with the rest of the Boer artillery, intended to pave the way for a two-pronged attack. Estimates of the number of attackers vary between 500 and 1,000. The force, however, was repelled. Altogether some 300 shells fell within the lines of investment.

3 The arrival of a relief-force was a constant subject of discussion. Any hopes at that time, however, must have been very remote as Colonel Plumer's regiment had been placed at Tuli near the Rhodesian border. Owing to the size and distance of his force, Plumer was in no position to attempt an attack on the besiegers. The arrival of troops from England had also been delayed.

4 Kanya (now officially spent 'Kanye') is the capital of the Bangwaketse tribe. It lies approximately sixty miles north-north-west of Mafeking.

5 Plaatje was a keen music lover and musician. In the diary this is reflected in his predilection for the use of musical metaphor.

6 The 'Staats Artillerie' were responsible for the operation of Boer artillery.

According to Grinnell-Milne (*Baden-Powell at Mafeking*, 1957, p. 106), many of these gunners 'were Germans lent from the Kaiser's army'.

7 The Molopo flows through the *stadt*. It appears from oral reports that Plaatje resided in a homestead near the river bank.

8 It has proved impossible to ascertain the surname of the man concerned. A survivor of the siege who knew Plaatje has proffered the information that David was the diarist's 'cousin' (the exact genealogical relationship is unclear as Barolong use this term to denote a variety of relationships of a classificatory nature), as well as his closest friend.

9 *Makasono* is the Tswana rendering of 'Maxim'. *Kgalema* literally translated means 'chide', 'scold', 'speak angrily' (J. Tom Brown, *Secwana–English Dictionary*, 1931). The use of the vernacular here is not arbitrary. It reflects a common Barolong linguistic practice. When speaking English, Tswana words which have – for the speaker – either an onomatopoeic quality or greater descriptive suitability are used. *Makasono* has a staccato quality that is missing from its less descriptive English equivalent, and the *kg-* (*kgalema*) represents a hard sound (ejective velar fricative) which is appropriate when used to indicate the implied emotion.

10 This is often used by Plaatje as shorthand to denote the Transvaal and Orange Free State republics.

11 Teacher Samson was a well-known Morolong and is sometimes (erroneously) cited as the first African teacher in Mafeking. The Barolong predilection for nicknaming explains why he is referred to as 'Teacher' rather than by his first name. Samson's homestead still stands in Mafikeng, and his fame is recalled at family gatherings even today.

12 This is used to denote an African township or village. The term subsequently became synonymous with African urban concentrations throughout South Africa. Here it refers to what was originally the Fingo village (see below).

13 These Fingoes came from a tribe which lives on the south-eastern plain of southern Africa. They had been recruited to travel north with Rhodes' Pioneer Column nine years earlier. However, on arriving at Mafeking, they chose to remain and establish a village outside the *stadt*. During the siege this settlement was known as the Fingo location. There was also an urban location outside Mafeking. This was populated by Africans of mixed ethnic origin (as opposed to the Barolong village which was almost exclusively Tswana). This location existed until 1967, when its population was moved into the newly constructed Montshiwa Township. Unless otherwise specified, 'location' (in both text and notes) refers to the urban strangers' location and not the Fingo village.

14 These lay a mile out of the town as it was then constituted. As they were situated in the area of the line of investment, the territory was disputed throughout the siege. It subsequently became the scene of several skirmishes.

15 The population of the *stadt* used the river for purposes of sanitation in those days. Even today, with the availability of borehole water, many women prefer to do their laundry (and gossiping) at the river bank.

16 This ultimatum is not referred to in other siege records. Nor is it clear which were the prior ultimata. Perhaps he is alluding to the letter sent by General Cronje to Colonel Baden-Powell on the evening of 20 October in which the former gave a forty-eight-hour forewarning of his intention to bombard the town, and added: 'You have to see that noncombatants leave Mafeking before the expiration of that time. If you do not comply with this I will not be answerable for the results.'

17 The Creusot siege-gun.

18 This village, also known as Rietfontein, is occupied by the Barolong boo

Rapulana, who allied themselves with the Boers. Properly spelt Lotlhakane, it is approximately twelve miles south of Mafeking.

19 Such troop movements were common during this period of the siege, for Cronje hoped to open a path into the town through heavy artillery-bombardment, followed by mounted attacks on weak points in the ring of defensive forts. That this was known to the besieged seems to indicate that at this time it was fairly easy to break the lines for intelligence purposes.

20 This is one of several names given to the Creusot siege-gun. The Boers termed it 'Gritje'. The British, who found this difficult to pronounce, called it 'Creechy' – which later developed into 'Creaky'. 'Big Ben' and 'Au Sanna' were two appellations the source of which is not clear. Plaatje prefers the last, and uses the name throughout the journal.

21 Makane was apparently the Serolong name for the Cannon Kopje area (see map). It is no longer used.

22 Dutch: 'pedestrian', 'hopper', 'wingless locust', 'infantry' (Kritzinger, Steyn, Cronje and Schoonees, *Groot Woordeboek*, 1937). Plaatje, again using the most evocative term available – and obviously intending irony by referring deprecatingly to the Boers in their own language – probably had the last meaning in mind.

23 This gives the impression that the Boers and Barolong were constantly at war, which is perhaps an overstatement. They spent much time in verbal debate and mutual cattle-raiding but only fought in 1853 at Lotlhakane (after which Montshiwa and most of his followers fled to Moshaneng, near Kanye; the remainder, under Molema, founded Mafeking), again in 1881 (Sehuba) and in 1882 (Mafeking).

24 This refers to the war of 1881 in which the Rapulana-Barolong, dissatisfied by Montshiwa's attempts to exert jurisdiction over them, recruited the help of the Barolong boo Ratlou and a group of burghers, and forced the chief to remove from Sehuba to Mafeking (a distance of nine miles). It was as a result of this that Molema's village became the Tshidi-Barolong capital, and that land was given by the successful chiefs to the burghers to found the Republic of Goshen (at Rooigrond, eleven miles away). After Montshiwa fled to Mafikeng he *did* successfully resist attacks on the town (mounted by the same allies) during 1882.

25 Everyone was acutely aware that the battle was crucial to the fate of Mafeking. Baden-Powell deployed supportive artillery which played a major part in the successful defence. Plaatje is probably trying to say that nobody cared to go to their assistance because of the strategic danger involved.

26 Estimates of the number of defenders in the Cannon Kopje (Makane) fort vary widely, and no two sources agree. Plaatje's estimate of seventy is the highest. In his diary J. Angus Hamilton (*Siege of Mafeking*, 1900, p.99) states that the defence was 'a mere gun emplacement and forty-four men . . .' Major F. D. Baillie's diary (*Mafeking*, p. 40) claims that the force was 'fifty-seven strong', while Grinnell-Milne (*Baden-Powell at Mafeking*, p. 91) puts the number at fifty.

27 Common among all parties was the strategy of 'playing dead' until the cover of night made escape possible. This ruse is frequently mentioned both in written records and by survivors. Apparently there existed a widespread dread of capture as stories about the treatment of prisoners on both sides emphasised a horror of this fate.

28 This spelling, like that for much of the vernacular in the text, is a function of the orthographic confusion of the era. *Thota*-ing (Sotho) or *Thutha*-ing (Xhosa-Zulu) is intended. It means 'carry' or 'transport'. The English suffix *-ing* is clearly

meant as a joke. Humour through word-play is a characteristic of the text, as it is of the author's cultural background.

29 Here again figures vary. That two officers (Captains Marsham and Pechell) were killed is, however, certain.

30 Plaatje's esteem for Captain Marsham was shared both by the garrison and by the beleaguered citizenry, Major Baillie (*Mafeking*, 1900, p. 40) predicted that, even among the enemy, regret over his death would be widespread, for his popularity was not limited by the line of investment. Much was made of the gallantry of his death, for it is reported that he died while assisting a wounded comrade.

31 The importance of this battle has, perhaps, been underplayed by the diarist. The military strategists among the defenders were quite aware that Cannon Kopje was at one and the same time a vital and a weak link in the defences. Being the highest point in the area it had clear vantage over the town, and all were adamant that, had it fallen, Mafeking would have become indefensible. It has subsequently been suggested that this incident might have become a turning-point in the war. This approach suggests that if the Boer forces that were tied up at Mafeking had been freed to reinforce other regiments elsewhere in the country before troops arrived from England, a powerful – if not irresistible – momentum might have developed. That Cannon Kopje was a weak link in the defences is explained by the fact that, in order to render it impregnable, it would have been necessary to blast away some of the rock of which the hill is entirely constituted. The rush to prepare the town's more immediate defence needs, it is argued, made it impossible to attend to this post before the siege was laid. Furthermore, dynamite was at the time a scarce commodity, for with it Baden-Powell created an important ruse: he ordered the burying of boxes in the ground along the perimeter and spread the word (the spies in Mafeking being particularly useful in this regard) that a mine-field had been planted. This might explain, to some extent, why Cannon Kopje was under-fortified.

32 This refers to the Cannon Kopje battle. Murchison commanded the artillery that supported the defenders from south of the Molopo, attacking the Boer flank with seven-pounder shells.

33 Parslow was the war correspondent of the *Daily Chronicle*. He was also to have assisted Whales, the editor of the *Mafeking Mail*, whose first siege-edition came out on this day. (It was subsequently issued daily, 'shells permitting'.) For reasons much speculated upon but never disclosed, Murchison shot the journalist through the head. He was later condemned to death by a court martial, but this sentence was commuted to life penal servitude by Lord Roberts on the advice of Baden-Powell.

34 In the capacity of interpreter and typist.

35 It must be remembered that the siege took place during the rainy season. Barolong, who depended largely on the elements for the success of their agricultural and pastoral activities, tend to worry obsessively about the weather. In this Plaatje is no exception – as later entries will prove.

36 The Kgalagadi were once thought of by ethnologists as impoverished Batswana who had taken to the desert when the other Tswana tribes migrated into eastern Botswana. While the latter is true, it has come to light that they are a separate division of the Sotho-speaking group of peoples. Traditionally some of their number formed (along with the Sarwa bushmen) a class of serfs among the stronger Tswana tribes. Today, however, they are simply commoners in these tribes. (See Schapera, *The Tswana*, 1953; Kuper, *Kalahari Village Politics*, 1970.)

37 The Women's Laager (Dutch: 'encampment') was set up some distance from

54

the town itself in order to concentrate the beleaguered women and children at a site safe from shelling. As no one envisaged that the siege would be lengthy, the encampment always remained temporary in its structure. Although most women sought safety in the Laager, some preferred to remain in town. The encampment was set up on the instruction of Colonel Baden-Powell.

38 *Laar* in this context is an abbreviated form of the word *laager*.

39 The Creusot siege-gun was often fired in the evening at about nine o'clock. As this invariably was only one round it became known by the besieged populace as the 'good-night' shot. Plaatje, who obviously saw the irony in this, altered the appellation and throughout the diary refers to it as the gun's 'bad-night'.

40 The strategy of using the railway line to propel explosives at the enemy had been used before. At the beginning of the siege (13 October) the armoured train was loaded with dynamite, and two trucks allowed to run down an incline towards Boers who were engaged in pulling up the rails to the north of the town.

41 Jackal Tree was, throughout the siege, the most common position for the Creusot siege gun. Although this ninety-four-pounder was moved on several occasions, Jackal Tree was most advantageous as it put Cannon Kopje and the town within close range.

42 'Barolongs' is an erroneous usage, being a double plural. The Setswana class-two subjectival concord *ba-* itself represents the plural. This usage is, still today, common among Barolong. In fact, its origin dates back to early European contact, when the grammatical structure of the language had not been documented. Folk linguists claim that Barolong use began through the mimicking of Europeans.

43 The man alluded to was a cousin (i.e., father's brother's son) to the chief of the Tshidi-Barolong, Wessels Montshiwa. The Tshidi had a system of named age-regiments to which young men were recruited. One of the traditional functions of these was the waging of war. Each regiment had a leader who was a son or close agnatic kinsman of the chief. In the case of this regiment the leader was Paul.

44 Bell was the Resident Magistrate and during the siege became the Civil Commissioner. In the latter capacity he had, among other things, the important task of liaison with the Barolong. Both in this sphere and in court work Plaatje was his interpreter, and the two men enjoyed a close friendship.

45 Baden-Powell's letter to Cronje warned of 'regrettable retribution' if the Boers persisted in shelling the Women's Laager, the hospital and the convent. Cronje replied that he had fired upon the convent because the British had mounted guns in that building. Although the *Mafeking Mail* (9 November) denies that this was so, Mother Mary Stanislaus writes in her unpublished diary that there was, in fact, an artillery emplacement in the convent. Later this was explained by apologists on the British side by the fact that the Boers had persisted in shelling the building, despite warnings, and that therefore Baden-Powell was simply paying them back in kind. Throughout the siege this was a bone of contention, and a considerable amount of correspondence passed between the respective commanders over it.

46 The passage in parentheses is written in the margin and is incomplete.

47 This entry is written against the two dates and is undifferentiated.

48 Weil's Store made an important contribution to the survival of the besieged populace. Ben Weil had, with amazing foresight, laid in tremendous stocks of foodstuffs and other necessities before the siege. With the other local merchants he played a major rôle in solving Baden-Powell's greatest problem; their supplies, together with a railway consignment which had been held up in Mafeking before investment, provided an important source of food.

49 All efforts to find information on these two people have failed. Barolong dispatch-runners were very useful to the British garrison, for knowing the country intimately, they managed often to slip through the Boer lines and return with news both of the outside world and of enemy troop movements.

50 Situated approximately eighteen miles north-west of Mafeking, this village is occupied by Barolong of the same tribe as those in the besieged town.

51 Ga-molimola (or Modimola) is also a Barolong boo Ratshidi village. It is thirteen miles due west of Mafeking.

52 I.e., the headman.

53 This paragraph is lightly crossed out in the original text. The incident to which the diarist refers is the arrival of the Warren Expedition in the district in early 1885. For several years before there had been land disputes between Boer and Barolong (see footnotes to the 31 October entry). Cecil Rhodes, then British Deputy Commissioner in Bechuanaland, advised the British Government to send a strong force 'to restore order in Bechuanaland and to defend the Native tribes who had placed themselves under British protection'. (Matthews, 'Short History of the Tshidi-Barolong', 1945, p. 20.) The Warren Expedition dispersed the citizens of the Goshen Republic but there is no reference to reparations or return of cattle in the available literature. Plaatje thus raises an interesting historical point. (For full accounts of this incident, see Matthews, 'Short History of the Tshidi-Barolong', 1945; Molema, *Montshiwa*, 1966.)

54 Stephen Lefenya, who held the position of secretary to Chief Montshiwa and his successors, was an important personality in tribal affairs. He later became a chiefly emissary and often negotiated with both British and Boers on matters affecting the tribe.

55 These are 'farms' owned by the Barolong in what was then the Bechuanaland Protectorate. (See Schapera, 'The System of Land Tenure on the Barolong Farms', 1943.)

56 The entire entry is lightly deleted, for no apparent reason. The insertion in parentheses is written in pencil at the top of the relevant page. Already a habitual manipulator of language for the sake of humour, he appears to be experimenting with alliteration.

57 This was the home of the Resident Commissioner, Mr C. G. H. Bell.

58 This must have been the Tswana name given by the Barolong to some or other Boer leader. The prefix *ra* (properly *rra*) here means 'father', though it may be used, very broadly, in relation to any adult male. *Ntho'akgale* (Sotho-Tswana) is a combinative term – *ntho* being a 'bruise', 'sore' or 'leprosy' and *akgale* meaning 'of the past'. Thus the nickname personified by the prefix *rra* may be translated as 'an old sore'. Its derogatory nature reflects the fact that the Barolong saw the Boer commanders as long-time enemies. Barolong living in Mafikeng today could not recall the appellation; but it probably refers to Cronje, who had been involved in previous Boer-Barolong dispute.

59 A small African child. This word – the linguistic origins of which are not clear – has become a South African colloquialism. Its use here gives us an insight into Plaatje's study of literary style. On Monday, the 13th, we saw how he experimented with alliteration. 'The pate of a piccaninny' is a contrived phrase which the author introduces – almost self-consciously, it seems – in order to give expression to a newly acquired literary technique. As elsewhere, we see here the function of the diary as an exercise in the study of literary skills, and watch Plaatje, the scholar, maturing.

60 A small village with grazing-lands, some two miles to the west of the *stadt*.

61 The war correspondents sent to Mafeking were G. N. Whales (Cape Press), who also edited the *Mafeking Mail*, Vere Stent (Reuter), J. E. Neilly (*Pall Mall*

*Gazette*), J. Angus Hamilton (the London *Times*) and F. D. Baillie (the *Morning Post*). Plaatje's services, as typist and interpreter, would have been in demand among these men for whom secretarial help must have been in short supply.

62 Mr E. G. Parslow, the deceased correspondent of the *Daily Chronicle*.

63 The alarm system worked as follows: whenever sentries observed the gunners elevating the barrel of 'Big Ben' someone was sent off to ring the alarm bells. This gave the townspeople a few minutes to take cover. The Boers, however, learnt of this, and after readying the gun, left it for a while. As a result the warning-system became less reliable.

64 The ninety-four-pounder.

65 General Cronje actually left on the 18th. According to Grinnell-Milne (*Baden-Powell at Mafeking*, 1957, p. 109) he took 6,000 men with him, leaving the succeeding commander, Snyman, with 4,000. The departure of Cronje signalled the beginning of a new strategy on the part of the Boers.

66 There is no report of this elsewhere, and either the diarist is the only one to record the incident, or he was misled by the fact that the gun was moved to a new position on the 17th.

67 All figures show evidence of multiple alteration in the text.

68 This sentence is phrased clumsily in the text. The editor has taken the liberty of rewording it in order to render it comprehensible.

69 St Leger was the author's eldest son. Like his mother, he had not accompanied Plaatje to Mafeking.

70 Mr Molema was a descendant of the founder of Mafeking. One of the Tshidi-Barolong nobility, his son married Plaatje's youngest daughter some years later.

71 He appeared before the court again the next day and, owing to lack of evidence, was convicted of improper, rather than treasonable, conduct (*Mafeking Mail*, 25 November).

72 When the siege began Baden-Powell declared martial law in the town. I have not, however, been able to find a clear statement of the division of functions between its different courts. It was not simply a matter of courts martial dealing with judicial matters among the militia and the Court of Summary Jurisdiction handling civilian misdemeanours. The latter often sat before military men (especially Major Goold-Adams, Colenel C. B. Vyvian and Major Lord Edward Cecil) while the Preliminary Examination in the Parslow murder case was heard by the Resident Magistrate, C. G. H. Bell. Only later was that trial transferred to a Field General Court Martial. Roughly speaking, however the division of labour did fall along the lines of the military or civilian status of the accused. Plaatje worked for the Court of Summary Jurisdiction as a (Dutch-English-Setswana) translator and later as a shorthand secretary.

73 Entries from the 24th to the 26th are written in a completely different handwriting. This second style appears again later on in the diary. Plaatje offers no explanation for it, but as these passages are notable for the frequency of spelling errors and lack of punctuation it is possible that he dictated them to someone who wrote them for him. The style and content, however, are unmistakably Plaatje's.

74 'Close up' probably means parting or final (in this case, shot).

75 We can only guess that by 'cut down below' the diarist means 'dead'. 'Bud' refers to Mr I. Bud Mbelle, brother-in-law and friend of Plaatje. As the diarist had worked as a court interpreter, it is likely that he had known — and, perhaps, befriended — the Judge President.

# 2   December 1899

## Friday, 1st

A very lovely morning after the last two days rain. I have lately said that all of the small artillery appears to have left us but I see that in this I was grossly mistaken as the one pounder Maxim is sounding out there and there are two other 7-pounders besides the one that had always been there. We had trying entertainment from the whole lot, but they are not of much account.

## Saturday, 2nd

We received a lot of news today – by people from across the border and also from a dispatch rider. The latter is Freddy No. 2. He is a member of the Lefenya family and was out to Kuruman.[1] On his arrival there he found the Cape Police in the Seoding Camp, beleaguered. The missionary (Reverend J. T. Brown), who had the 'Vierkleur'[2] waving over his dwelling-house would not even look at him, but drove him away directly he learned that the man was from Mafeking and absolutely declined to tell him which was the safer way into the Boer surrounded camp. He, however, delivered his dispatches and on his way back called at Ganyesa,[3] where he was caught and searched by the Boers, who on finding these letters on him took him to Vryburg. They reached there in the night and he escaped under cover of the dark while they were busy reading his dispatches. He returned to Ganyesa that very same night and on the following day interpreted for his pursuers in an interview with the Chief Lethlogile.[4] The Chief, on being asked with which side his sympathies were, said he sympathises with no one and was quite neutral from the fight but he was only going to side with the winning side at the end of the trouble – clever fellow.

The smaller artillery round us have just arrived. I wonder whether the Boers still imagine that we are afraid of the 7-pounder, for the lot of them put together are not half, nay, even quarter, of 'Au Sanna'.[5] Therefore after 6 weeks under 94-pound shells it is folly to think any number of 5- and 7-pounders would knock anything out of us.

From across the border we learn that it is quite true that we silenced 2 of the enemy's guns on the 23rd[6] and that the following is the result of the season's fixtures between Baden-Powell's 400 [7] and Cronje's 10 times that number:

| Baden-Powell | 287 | What a licking! |
|---|---|---|
| Cronje | 19 | |

Mind you this does not include the fight on October 14th and the bayoneting on October 21st. Those games were against the Snyman and Botha teams called the Marico Commando — exclusive of Cronje who only fought on the occasion of the all-round attack of October 25th, the attack on Makane on October 31st and the morning of Tuesday 7th Ultimo.

P.S. I have allowed Cronje too much: he did not score 19. 7 were scored by the Marico Laager, 7 by Cronje at the Makane game — 31st October — and the big gun is responsible for the balance.

### Sunday, 3rd

This is the Lord's day. All deadly instruments have been laid aside and we are now thinking of the Goodness of the All-Father and his immeasurable wisdom in preserving for himself the seventh day that all men should worship. I wonder how we should be if that was not the case. When the week rolls past and we find ourselves alive on Friday morning we congratulate ourselves as we will only have two days more before the blessed Sabbath, on which we will get rid of the horrible thunder for a day. There is only one thing we are particular about and that is not to stray too far from within the 'lappiegrond'[8] forming the perimeter of Mafeking between us and the enemy's lines, as this is disputed territory. It is really touching to see ladies and children from the Women's Laager (where Mr H. Whiteley, the Mayor,[9] had been their Good Shepherd for all the week) meet their brothers, husbands, fathers, etc. from the trenches. From Monday to Saturday our beleaguered home has the appearance of Judgement Days, while today it looks like a gay Christmas. There were all kinds of sports today; gymkhana, turf, band and concerts.

### Monday, 4th

When I reached town this morning I found that dispatches had arrived. They bring news of Kimberley having been successfully relieved [10] on the 23rd Ultimo, by a force of three thousand Troops and that Lord Methuen was coming up with ten thousand more men.

Kimberley, which we thought had been relieved about a month ago, had only just been relieved on the St Leger's birthday. He was surely going to have a grand birthday if he happened to be there.

We had only three shots from 'Sanna' in the forenoon and none in the afternoon. While still jotting down these notes I looked at my time-piece to find that it was 9.33: 'Sanna's' 'bad-night' always came between 8.00 and 9.00 so I was saying to David that the old dame is not going to 'lumelisa'[11] today.

I had hardly finished when 'bang' went a terrible report, a sharp loud hum, and then a blood-stirring explosion and other reports when the deadly fragments proceeded to complete their various missions. This is an abominable life.

There is an item about Linchwe[12] having surprised a lot of Boers, captured cattle, horses, wagons, Mausers and a lot of women. The latter were returned to their sweethearts as surely as aught else was detained. Women are not of any value in war. Only Boers view the subject differently. Kgakgamaco and Sinobe were coming from Modimola the other day and were fired on by Boers. Only the previous week some women were coming in from the same place. They carried bundles on their heads and the Boers shot a bundle off one head. The stubbornness of Barolonghazi[13] is extraordinary. They stopped, picked up the bundle and calmly loaded it again. 'Baka ba bolaea fela.'[14]

An officer of the Protectorate Regiment sent his wife to Mosita for safety. She afterwards went to Setlagoli as Boers were visiting Mosita almost daily. She subsequently found Setlagoli intolerable and decided to go up to the Boers and ask them for a permit to come into Mafeking. The Boers detained her at the Laager and sent word to Baden-Powell that they could only release Her Ladyship provided one Pietrus Viljoen (a prisoner undergoing nine months hard labour for theft) is allowed to go to the Laager. I wonder what will be the end of the correspondence.[15]

*Tuesday, 5th*

I had a busy time today. A white man was charged with committing rape on a Native girl. The police rescued her off him and made a prisoner of him. I interpreted in this case and just when the evidence was about to reach the filthiest, superior authorities (military) demanded my services and I departed only to return towards the conclusion when the interpreting in it had become quite ceremonious. The military court cares nought for any such cases: I believe we will keep the evidence until the roads are open and commit him for trial before the judge next quarter.

I did not return to town this afternoon, the heaviest rain of the season having graced us with a visit. Surely if things go on at this rate the few, with whose ploughing the effects of this war did not interfere, will have too much grain for house consumption. The shower was heavy but quiet – so quiet that I fell asleep and only woke at 4.10 p.m. to find the village in flood. As I happened to be away in dreamland, and do not know what took place, I will leave the *Mafeking Mail* to describe the affair:

Dead puppies, stinking sprats, all drenched in mud, drowned cats and turnip tops came tumbling down the flood' is what Dean Swift said in his description of a city shower. We suppose from his mentioning dead puppies and drowned cats that he meant it was raining 'cats and dogs'. We don't know the origin of the 'cats and dogs' shower but, if its root is 'kata doros' as some learned writer suggested or 'contrary to experience' we think it rained 'cats and dogs' yesterday. A sprinkle of over eight inches in about one hour is decidedly contrary to experience. Fortunately we are so positioned that there is ample natural drainage to take away even the enormous quantity of water which fell yesterday, but the trenches were soon filled and from them the water could not run. More damage to property was done by the storm than the Boers could ever accomplish in their 'storming'. Rations were destroyed, kits washed away, and in one case a man was nearly drowned, or smothered in the mud. He slipped in, fortunately feet downwards, and had not two of his companions been near him and promptly 'hauled him back again' he would have been done for. At the Hospital Redan [16] the underground kitchen was flooded with six feet of water, the dinner beef spoiled and various little 'extras' the men had subscribed to buy, were lost. The Women's Laager trench was an underground canal. The Sisters [17] were washed out from their 'bomb-proof' and the Cape Police had an hour's diving in the seven feet deep coffee coloured pool for Maxim ammunition; while everyone had an experience of wetness and discomfort, which it is to be hoped will remain unique, but which was borne by the whole garrison in the same cheery manner which has been shown during all the time of the Siege. We hope our friend the enemy enjoyed himself, and to help cheer him up we should like to tell him that through his lack of nous and pluck he missed a chance yesterday to annoy us, which is never likely to present itself again.[18]

Some people had been over to the Boer lines to 'thiba'[19] cattle. They managed to get four – abnormally fat elephants. They gave one to the chief, slaughtered two, ate part of the meat, and retailed the balance. I did not avail myself of the opportunity of finding out what loot tastes like as Meko had slaughtered a fat hammel and the hard ox is not very desirable when palatable mutton is knocking about.

## Wednesday, 6th

Went to town for a while in the morning then visited the Meko's whose children are very ill. At 3 p.m. I went to see Vere Stent [20] on business. He left the hole and we settled for a chat in the open air when we were unsettled by a loud bang just at old Gerrans' blacksmith shop exactly opposite where we were. We looked and saw things mighty gloomy in the blacksmith shop: grown-up folks screaming in the dark smoke like piccaninnies after 'kgoathaing',[21] while old Gerrans could be seen walking about in front of the shop, his face as black as that of a corner man in McAddo's Vaudevilles.[22] It turned out to be an explosion of an originally unexploded shell, which had been picked up and sold to som:one and the purchaser, like all others, took it to poor Mr Gerrans to empty the fuse and the powder. Mr Gerrans had been doing many of them and as there are exceptions in all cases, this particular one stood no molestation but burst with the vigour of a shell direct from 'Sanna', knocked poor Mr Gerran's left-hand fingertips off, blackened his face with powder, tore his trousers and vests to pieces besides 'other wrongs and injuries'. As for Mr Green his assistant, it went for his leg (its favourite part) so severely that it had to be amputated; but an unfortunate person, a refugee from Johannesburg, named Smith, happened to be passing in front of the scene of this outburst just at the time of the explosion and had both his legs so fearfully battered that he was only able to scream at the start. When I reached there he lay quite quiet and the poor fellow died shortly after.

One shell hit Mr Weil's store yesterday. The store was full of customers and shop employees. It entered through the roof, travelled between the roof and the ceiling, shattering the beams until it destroyed the ceiling and exited through the wholesale door. Fragments made a race for the railway station. During that race a Burghersdorp chap – a refugee from Johannesburg – came in contact with one and was killed. The crowd in the shop escaped without injury. Another shell came round in the afternoon. It entered the private house of our young Town Clerk, pierced the outer wall and went on to a room in which the Town Clerk was. It destroyed the room and wrecked everything inside except the Town Clerk – a marvellous escape: one fragment went to the kitchen, where the cook, a very stout bastard [23] lady, was and shook her so vehemently that she nearly had the perfect circulation of her blood disorganised.

## Thursday, 7th

A lovely morning. After I got up I rode in the direction of Meko's to inquire where last night's shot fell, as it burst in the Stadt. I found that it had fallen on the ground near a wagon wheel to which a cow was tied, whence the broken shell made for the cow, dispatched it to eternity, splintered the strong wagon and severely wounded a chappie that was playing on the other side of it. Bits of the cow's meat were scattered in every direction. When I was there, shelling proceeded very briskly from 'Sanna' and the smaller artillery which are of minor importance. Only 'Sanna' is our 'ingwe'.[24] I went up to town and just after I crossed the railway line, the alarm bells chimed. The pony knows them already and he became infuriated and bucked like a damn cow while I tried to make him stand on the lee of Whiteley, Walker & Co's store. He was still bucking when a shell flew overhead with a sharp loud hum and burst in the direction of the railway. Things were too serious to permit of a fellow hanging about the streets of Mafeking and I turned round the Stadt way as fast as his legs could carry me. The next shell burst just as I reached the outskirts of the village.

During my short stay in town I learned that the first shell of this morning burst near one of the railway cottages and killed a young fellow by blowing off his belly and pitching his intestines onto the opposite roof.

The man Phil-june [25] has been allowed to go so Lady Sarah Wilson reached here this morning. She says the Boers at the Laager say that their forces are slaying 1,000's of the English everywhere – at least so they are told – but they are puzzled as to how Lord Methuen managed to reach Kimberley if that was the case.

I wonder why the Boers are so 'kwaai'[26] today. During the last few days we seldom had a 'Sanna' shell during the forenoon, and then a day's complement was only between 2 and 4, but this morning we had 7 between 7.00 a.m. and 8.00 a.m. from 'Sanna' only, besides a heavy thunder from the smaller artillery and a shower of Mauser which played the accompaniment. The middle of the day was somewhat quiet but operations were resumed at 3.30 p.m. with great vigour. I was obliged to stop going to town this afternoon despite urgent private affairs. The afternoon fire lasted till sunset but 'Sanna', just to show that she is older and mightier than the lot, kept up her part as long as the moon was shining – till 8.30 p.m. It will be a serious business if the Boers are going to give us no more sleep while the moon is shining. We always had only one shell – the 'bad-night' shot – fired into us between 8.00 and 9.00 p.m.

This single one we find very inconvenient as it makes everyone imagine, at sunset, that he is either going to have his legs shattered or a few nambulatory [27] escapes – if he is not annihilated to death; but if we are going to have them as regularly as we had them this day we might as well expect to be throwing up the sponge soon. Our patience is altogether exhausted. When the trouble commenced no-one dreamt that we would still be beleagured at the end of November: others gave the Troops only up to 30th October to arrive here; I, however, gave them up to 30 October to reach Kimberley and to arrive there on 20th November, which was about the most liberal of the lot. But here were are today, December 7th, losing people daily and not even able to tell where the Troops are. Surely if everybody knew that this was going to be the case we would never have had the forebearance to start it. The result of yesterday afternoon's 'Sanna' outrage was 2 whites and a native killed, and 2 whites wounded. If we are going to die at this rate I am sure there will only be wounded people hopping about single armed and with amputated legs to tell the History of the Siege.

One of the killed was in Mr Riesle's bar (Mafeking Hotel). They are dead against our poor ex-Mayor: when they shelled us with 12- and 7-pounders, on the 16th October, Mr Riesle was the only person who got his window smashed; I have already described how they went for his sitting-room and wrecked the piano and goods therein being, but have not mentioned that when 'Sanna' (before she was christened) gave her début in Mafeking on October 23rd Mr Riesle was the first victim. It went for him in a quaint manner; some flames had to be put out, which has never been the case with any other explosion up till this day. They have since been going for his outhouses, back-cottages, servants' rooms and W.C.'s time after time in a most merciless manner. I have never before realised so keenly that I am walking on the brink of the grave. It is really shocking, while still meditating how one of your fellow creatures met his fate at the shell of the Dutch cannon, to hear that many more had their legs and 'sinqes' [28] shattered somewhere; and it is an abominable death to be hacked up by a 94-pounder. People say the reason is that shells being less frequent, the inhabitants are less particular about taking the necessary precautions. I, however, attributed the ludicrous failure of 'Sanna' during the months of October and November to the fact that people were considerably alarmed, and sighed to their Creator – of whose possession they were then perfectly certain – nearly every second. Their soliloquies were so far retrenched by the perilousness of their position that in their cogitation there was only room for the one word 'God'; and they yearned for the company of His Angels more than they cared to meditate sin. But now we have so far forgotten ourselves as to imagine that this failure was attributable not to Providential Protection but to Cronje's misfortune and our good luck, or to his cowardice and our valour – what an odd notion.

*Friday, 8th*

We rose in high spirits preparing for a heavy day's shelling. We wonder whether yesterday's rapid outburst was because they received a fresh supply of ammunition or that Phil-june told them that they had just begun to do damage; but they only hit harder. During the day only an occasional Mauser and about six bangs from their thinner artillery kept us cognisant of the fact that we are beleaguered. What a contrast to unfortunate yesterday.

As a rule the 'Native Question' has, I believe, since the abolition of slavery, always been the gravest question of its day. The present Siege has not been an exception to this rule for Natives have always figured pre-eminently in its chief correspondence. The following letter is public property and I have decided on reproducing it [29] in extenso:

Mafeking, 8th Dec., 1899.

To General Snyman,
    near Mafeking.

Sir, — I beg to thank you for having handed over Lady Sarah Wilson in exchange for the convict P. Viljoen.

At the same time, I beg to point out that I have only consented to the exchange under protest,[30] as being contrary to the custom of civilised warfare.

In treating this lady as a prisoner of war, as well as in various other acts, you have in the present campaign, altered the usual conditions of war. This is a very serious matter; and I do not know whether it has the sanction of General Joubert or not, but I warn you of the consequences.

The war was at first, and would remain, as far as Her Majesty's troops are concerned, a war between one Government and another; but you are making it one of people against people in which women are considered as belligerents. I warn you that the consequence of this may shortly be very serious to your own people, and you yourself will be to blame for anything that may happen.

Regarding your complaint as to your being attacked by Natives I beg to refer you to my letter dated 14th November, addressed to your predecessor, General Cronje. In this letter I went out of my way, as one white man to another, to warn you that the Natives are becoming extremely incensed at your stealing their cattle, and the wanton burning of their Kraals; they argued that the war lay only between our two Nations, and that the quarrel had nothing to do with themselves, and they had remained neutral in consequence, excepting in the case of the Mafeking Baralongs, who had to defend their homes in consequence of your unjustifiable invasion. Nevertheless, you thought fit to carry on cattle theft and raids against them, and you are now beginning to feel the consequences; and, as I told you, I could not be responsible. And I fear from what I have just heard by wireless telegraph that the Natives are contemplating further operations should your Forces continue to remain within or on the borders of their territories. Before the commencement of the war the High Commissioner issued stringent orders to all Natives that they were to remain quiet and not to take up Arms unless their territory were invaded (in which case, of course, they had a perfect right to defend themselves).

Linchwe – of whom you complain – remained neutral until you brought a force into his principal town and looted his traders' stores, and were making preparations for shelling his stadt on the 26th ultimo. Having obtained accurate information of these intentions of yours and, warned by what had happened to the Natives near Mafeking, he attacked your laager on the 24th in order to save his town from being shelled and consequent loss of life amongst his women and children. In this I consider he was quite justified, and you have no one but yourself to blame in the matter.

While on the subject of Natives please do not suppose that I am ignorant of what you have been doing with regard to seeking the assistance of armed natives, nor of the use of the Natives by you in the destruction of the railway line south of Mafeking. However, having done my duty in briefly giving you warning on these points, I do not propose to further discuss them by letter.

I have the honour to be,

Sir,

Your obedient servant,

R. S. S. BADEN-POWELL, Col.

'Au Sanna' seems to have been blessed now. The only shot she discharged today did considerable damage. It came at 1.25, just when I was returning from town. It cut across my track and went for the B.S.A. Camp in a most sickening whizz. It entered the stable and found several men of the Protectorate Regiment attending their horses; killed one and wounded two. The dead man was singing at the time it went for him.

It is marvellous that while we had 'Sanna's' shells at the rate of 50 per diem, besides hundreds from the thinner artillery, we lost no-one; but now nearly every one of her shots kills a man and injures several. I am more keen about my impression of yesterday. People have started football, cricket and polo matches in defiance of shells. The Sunday is a day of gymkhana meetings and merryments which serve as strong counter-attractions to Divine Services. These surely must be one of the causes of the deadliness of the Dutch weapons now. I had entered my pony for a run in next Sunday's races – everybody who knows him was very sanguine that he would take the prize, but I had decided to withdraw him today lest I be guilty of blatant sacrilege and thereby further imperil my already dangerous condition. Fancy, only one shot being fired during a very quiet day and carrying off three persons by a single stroke.

### Saturday, 9th

Too little, if anything, has been said in praise of the part played by that gallant Britisher – the Barolong herdboy. Cattle are now grazing on what may be termed 'disputed' territory, just where the Dutch and English volleys cross each other; and it is touching to see how piccaninnies watch their flocks, and how in the bright sunshine along the wide plain south and west of the Stadt – especially when after filling his belly with a lunch of black coffee and beef – the Dutch artillerist would turn his attention to them, and sate his iniquitous whims by sending a shell right in the midst of a group of them. God would guide it flying over their little heads and it would kindle a mortal fire near them: it is an imposing sight to see them each running after a fragment and calmly picking it up. They would quietly mind their stock or drive them home under a severe shell fire with the tenacity of the African in all matters where cattle are concerned. The chappie killed by that shell that struck the hospital last month was turning goats on the rushes at the back of the hospital. The Boers made a small retort within easy range of a Martini south of the Stadt. They had intended to snipe the Stadt from there, but the Stadt folks made it hot for them. Last week a few herds [31] went straight up to it [32] and brought home some tinned beef biltong and two spades.

Two other herds went out last night. They went out as far as Jackal Tree, where they lay down on the grass near the Boer camp, when the enemy were busy outspanning. It was raining at the time and the oxen were tied up to the yokes. They waited until the owners sheltered themselves from the rain, then advanced and successfully loosened four of the oxen without detection. One of the smart thieves led them away by their reims, [33] while his confederate drove their loot behind.

There is a regiment composed of a mixture of Zulu, Shangaan, Tembu and other Transkeian breeds under one Mackenzie, styled the Black Watch. These are camped just where the railway passes Bokone. [34] Some of these fellows on sentry duty saw their Barolong brethren advancing with their highly prized but 'nqabile' [35] possession. The party was mad and an eruption, such as nearly started a revolution in the whole place, ensued. Their row was such as could have attracted considerable attention if 'Au Sanna' was not the lawful claimant of our attention. The case was 'sticking up' [36] and the Colonel judged against the Transkeians, as the Barolong could substantiate their claims by the reims they carried in their hands. The Zulu swore that they brought the cattle from the Boer laager. The Colonel gave the Barolong the third ox and as they were abnormally fat animals he bought the others off them.

This cattle theft has put the Boers on the alert. On Thursday I sent out a man to Kimberley for Vere Stent; he and his companion tried to cross along the railway line but they found the country so excellently guarded by the Boers that to get through was an impossibility. They tried to north-west with the same result and they are now planning a scheme for a fresh try tomorrow. The Barolongs had a brush in miniature with the enemy this morning.

About 90 Boers were observed a half mile to the south of the Stadt waiting for our cattle. When the cattle were cleared away from the Stadt range the Boers stormed the herds, who finding it impossible to drive the cattle, ran home for arms. Uncle Cornelius happened to be about and he alone managed to keep the Boers until his bandolier was empty. Just then about 40 men came up and drove the Boers off. One of our men got a slight wound and the Boers wounded three cows and a donkey. We only hope we have given them something in return.

*Sunday, 10th*

The usual Holy holiday. No Mausering. We have not received any dispatch since last week, when we heard of the Relief of Kimberley. The story by our dispatch carrier that the Boer lines are impassable must be correct and this accounts for our not receiving any dispatches. Some three of our men have been to the Transvaal to loot cattle. They went out on Friday and slept at a farmhouse occupied only by poultry. They killed half a dozen fowls and supped on them. They stayed in a hole all day Saturday and in the evening advanced towards a Boer homestead which they had been espying during the day. One of them went to guard the door of the homestead, with his Martini well cocked, and ready to 'Quma' [37] – directly a Dutchman (or woman) put out his head – while the others went to empty a kraal of the fourteen heads of cattle that were in it. They took every one of them. They brought us some interesting news. While at the poultry-house they heard some voices in the dark, which they recognised as those of some of our Kalaharis [38] in Rietfontein (now Boer territory). These Kalaharis were from delivering some Dutch letters, at the Eastern Laager, and expressed regret at not having met our men prior to delivering them as they would have handed them over for our information and let the Boers 'sweat'. These Bakgalagalis reported having heard at the laager that there was a heavy fight between Kimberley and some river or other – probably the Vaal – towards the end of last moon (end of November) in which both sides lost heavily. The English lost 'vyf honderd' and the Dutch lost 'tien honderd'.[39] Our friend Mnr. Cronje was also there and his commando was scattered in every direction.

The usual gaiety and merryments took place in the afternoon.

There being no danger I took the pony and went out for a ride around 'disputed territory' and saw the Boers so close that I nearly felt inclined to go over and have a chat with them as they were seated on the ridges of their trenches looking at games played so merrily round our camp with longing eyes; this however is a serious crime and I cannot bring trouble upon myself in that manner. They undoubtedly wonder of what stuff we are made, to look so little the worse for this long Siege. I wonder whether they have forgotten that while Cape Town and many important colonial towns have been seats of Dutch governments and still wear Dutch names, Mafikeng [40] has since its creation never been cursed by being a Boer Laager, despite strenuous endeavours to make it such. It still bears the name given it by Tau's [41] band of Barolong who came from Lake Ngami in about 1750. They were a peaceful lot of men, yet they plundered everybody who dared interfere with their migration, and earned for themselves the title of 'Baga Rungoana le Bogale'.[42] To return to our subject: these West Transvaalians ought to remember that Mafeking has always held her own against becoming Dutch and the only Boer who ever owned Mafeking was the one who swore by the honour of the King. It is a pleasant day; fair and cloudy, with an occasional shower every now and then.

### Monday, 11th

I went to town early this morning to fetch Mr Hamilton to take pictures in our village for *Black and White*,[43] which paper he represents besides the London *Times*. A shell burst while I was at the Residency where I always feel comfortable even if the alarm bells go. It flew overhead and travelled for miles away in a north-westerly direction. I went to Riesle's for Hamilton and the bells rang while he was still preparing. The discomfort I endured can easily be imagined, for Riesle's is a place which I always hurry to pass quickly – even if there is nothing in the wind. It however went towards the railway and exploded there. We then left. Mr Briscoe's [44] drift is not the road to travel, being exposed to the eastern Mausers and shells, particularly when one is on horseback – so we went to cross by the missionaries' foot drift (Lekoko's New Dam). While we were in the plain between the town and our village we observed some heavy firing to the south of the Stadt: at the foot drift we were met by several women, who said they were nearly all hit by Mauser bullets while routing 'Lichachane'[45] for fuel. They had to come home minus the wood during a hail of bullets, every one of which fortunately missed them. When we reached Mr Lefenya's house, we showed the pressmen where lives my old uncle, who kept 90 Boers off on Saturday. I had scarcely finished when the old dame came to meet us and informed me that he had just come home wounded. With the prudence and forethought of the European, Mr Hamilton had every requisite with him and after we had dismounted we went in and washed and dressed the wound, which was, however, not very bad — having entered by the left armpit and exited through the fleshy part of the left breast, touching no bones. Little Tiego,[46] chief of the younger corps, had one of his left toes slightly tipped off and two other fellows were wounded, each in the leg — none dangerously. This gives one the idea that the Dutch muskets, unlike their artillery, have had their curses taken off, for this is really the Barolong's first casualty since the war broke out. I am afraid they have given the Boers nothing in return, for directly they got a sufficient view of the Boers the latter retreated hurriedly.

We received news that two dispatch runners were trying to come in here on Thursday night but were fired at by Boers. During their run for dear life the dispatches got lost and they have now gone back to Kanya. The man Samuel Lefenya, who cheated the Boers at Ganyesa a few days back, was leaving Mafeking with his wife. They were fired at by Boers and he got dangerously hit in the stomach; his wife was shot in the thigh and they were both taken to the Laager. The former is not expected to live. The Boers have been seen picking 130 men and horses for the purpose of reinforcing the north. They say the English are so numerous up there that it is feared they will build the line.[47]

The Boers must have thought that we were now eating horses and were surrendering, because of the white flags leaving for all of the trenches round about us. It was Colonel-Baden-Powell sending out copies of the accompanying circular [48] to the Burghers as he says it is exclusively for them and not for the officers and colonial rebels. It is a stirring manifesto, at least to me, but I wonder what its effects will be on Boer ears. We had a quiet day. Some rains set in during the forenoon.

NOTICE
TO THE BURGHERS OF THE Z.A.R.[49] AT PRESENT
UNDER ARMS NEAR MAFEKING.

From the Officer commanding His Majesty's Forces, Mafeking.

Burghers, — I address you in this manner because I have only recently learned how you are being intentionally kept in the dark by your officers and your Government newspapers as to what is really happening in other parts of South Africa.

As officer commanding His Majesty's troops on this border, I think it is right to point out to you clearly the inevitable result of your remaining any longer in arms against Great Britain.

You are all aware that the present war was caused by the invasion of British territory by your forces, and as most of you know, without justifiable reason.

Your leaders do not tell you that so far your forces have met with what is only the advanced guard of the British force, and that circumstances have changed within the past week; the main body of the British is now daily arriving by thousands from England, Canada, India and Australia, and is about to advance through your country. In a few weeks the South African Republic will be in the hands of the English; no sacrifice of life on your part can stop it. The question now put to yourselves before it is, is this: Is it worth while losing your lives in a vain attempt to stop their invasion or to take a town beyond your borders which, if taken, would be of no use to you? (And I may tell you that Mafeking cannot be taken by sitting down and looking at it, for we have ample supplies for several months to come.)

The Staat Artillery have done us very little damage, and we are now well protected with forts and mines. Your presence here, or elsewhere, under arms, cannot stop the British advancing into your country.

Your leaders and newspapers are also trying to make you believe that some foreign continental powers are likely to intervene on your behalf against England. This is not in keeping with their pretence that your side is going to be victorious, nor is it in accordance with the facts. The S.A.R. having declared war and taken the offensive cannot claim intervention on its behalf. And were it not so, the German Emperor is at present in England, and fully in sympathy with us: the American Government have warned others of their intervention on the side of England should any other nation interfere; France has large interests in the Gold Fields identical with those of England; and Italy is entirely in accord with us; and Russia sees no cause to interfere.

Your leaders have caused the destruction of farms in this country and have fired on women and children, and our men are becoming hard to restrain in consequence. Your leaders have also caused invasion of Kaffir territory, and looting of their cattle, and have thus induced them to rise, and in their turn to invade your country, and to kill your Burghers. As one white man to another, I warned General Cronje on the 14th November that this would occur, and yesterday I heard that more Kaffirs are rising, and are contemplating similar moves; and I have warned Snyman accordingly. Thus great bloodshed, and destruction of farms threaten you on all sides, and I wish to offer you a chance of avoiding it. To this end my advice to you is to return without delay to your homes and there remain peacefully until the war is over. Those of you who do this before the 14th instant will be as far as possible protected, as regards yourselves, your families, and property, from confiscations, lootings, and other penalties to which those who remain under arms may be subjected when invasion takes place.

Our secret agents will communicate to me the names of those who do and of those who do not avail themselves, before the 13th instant, of the terms now offered.

To ensure their property being respected, all the men of a family must be present at home when the troops arrive and be prepared to hand over a rifle and 150 rounds of ammunition each.

The above terms do not apply to officers or to members of the Staats artillery, who may surrender as prisoners of war at any time; nor do they apply to rebels from British territory or others against whom there may be other charges. It is probable that my force will shortly take the offensive.

To those who, after this warning, defer their submission till too late, I can offer no promise, and they will only have themselves to blame for any injury or loss of property that they or their families may afterwards suffer.

(Sgd.) R. S. S. BADEN-POWELL,

Colonel.

Mafeking, 10th December, 1899.

*Tuesday, 12th*

'Sanna' never moved till 5 p.m. when she sent five shells into the location. The thinner artillery and Mausers were very mild. We had a civil court today. A lot of boys of the firm of Julius Weil are suing their employers for wages. Mr Spencer Minchin L.L.B., solicitor (now Lieutenant Minchin, Bechuanaland Rifles), appeared for all the plaintiffs, and Mr L. W. de Kock, attorney (now member of the Town Guard), appeared for the defence. It was a novel court: only the parties concerned looked as usual, but not the court. The plaintiffs' attorney was in military attire; lawyer for the defence, never shaved since the Siege, all hairy and dressed in a third-hand suit without a collar, looked more like a farmer than an attorney. Myself in knickerbockers and without a jacket, looked more like a member of the football team or a village cyclist than a court interpreter. All of the natives, but one, carried their cases.

*Wednesday, 13th*

Boers held a big meeting in the forenoon, all hands attending. They are undoubtedly discussing Colonel Baden-Powell's manifesto. Anyhow it put a great change in the situation as they are not shooting in the forenoon any more. One good purpose it served is that they sent a newspaper to the Colonel probably to contradict his statement that their men are kept in the dark.[50] Besides what the Boers wished the Colonel to see in this paper (*Die Volkstem*, 7th December) it contained an account of a big fight at Modder River, in which Cronje, supported by some Free State Commandos, made a gallant stand against Lord Methuen.[51] The English, it says, had the worst of it as they had to advance in the open towards a well fortified opponent. They weakened the south flank and crossed the river and the Free Staters retired. Cronje held his fire well and was compelled to retire by the retreat of the Free Staters, who left their dead on the field and fled to Jakobsdal on the road to Bloemfontein. This is an excellent entertainment considering the long time we remained without news.

### Thursday, 14th

'Sanna' was quiet all the morning and commenced duty in the afternoon The first shot made straight for poor Sibale's house. It was full of people – women and children – including uninikazi,[52] Mrs P. Sidzumo. It pulled and shook the whole house upon them: pieces of shell or the house cut off her toes, shattered her leg and injured her face and head. The left leg was broken below the knee (and the thigh completely shattered). The other people remained alive in the debris. The poor husband, coming to see the remains of his house, was met with the ruins of his wife just pulled out of the debris. He became so senseless that he returned to the fort hardly knowing what he was doing until they told him that his wife wanted to see him. He jumped up in joyous bewilderment – for he had first imagined that she was dead already – and had a look at her before she was moved to the hospital. This was 3.45 and she died at 6.00 in the evening, leaving the husband and a little girl to mourn her loss.

We are very hard up for news. More dispatch runners went out last night but returned to say they found the Boer lines impassable. We had always received two dispatches every week. Now we have not received any for ten days and we really feel the strain.

Mrs P. Sidzumo was buried at 3 o'clock this morning. She had been in the Stadt yesterday afternoon and her husband came to call her back to the scene of yesterday's disaster.[53] They went to the location together. When her husband proceeded to the trench she remained at her ill-fated home, and waited unconcernedly for the hour of this sudden tragedy. The little girl is not cognisant of her bereavement and plays about well at her Granny's place.

There was a fight at the Natal border in which General Joubert's forces were completely disorganised and large numbers of them killed, General Joubert himself being taken prisoner.

We have heretofore received nearly all our news by telegraph, from the Boer Laager, whence it was conveyed by our people into Mafeking.[54] Mistakes have, of course, been made with regard to names, locations and numbers of casualties, but they may be excused on that score as they are no mathematicians or scholars of any kind. Now even if Joubert himself is not caught we will say that it is somebody and that it is some very important personage whose arrival deserves considerable fuss in the Transvaal.

Even the *Mafeking Mail*, which regards the native as a mere creature, was this day wont to say: 'Although the following statements from Native sources may only be rumour retailed, so many of the reports brought to hand through similar intelligence have been corroborated by official report received some weeks later, that we feel disposed to give more credence to a Kaffir ipse dixit than we formerly have done.' [55]

Anyhow if official intelligence is to be relied upon there were, at the end of last month, 10,000 Troops in Ladysmith and General Buller was advancing with 25,000 more. If truth is not stranger than fiction, what then prevents such large armies from catching the old General? [56]

I cannot make out why we are not getting any dispatches, for we have people other than letter-carriers going out and coming in. There must be something radically wrong in it.

### Monday, 18th

This has been an exceptionally quiet day. 'Au Sanna' never moved at all. Only the thinner artillery and a few Mausers 'shook the dust off their feet' a little. This is the first Siege holiday 'Sanna' gave us since her début on the 23rd October – about 3 months ago.

We received some news on Sunday but still we would not object to more, particularly since what we received was not in black and white. The 'Liar' had a very interesting item [57] to cheer us up, but as we could test the authenticity of this with our field glasses, we instantly flung it back in his face with thanks.

Two fellows were seen on disputed territory this morning. They were arrested and pleaded that they had left but last night in order to 'hamba inkomo',[58] which job they had found too tough. They saw, they said, seven loaded wagons leaving 'Sanna's' fort for Johannesburg during the night. One of the wagons contained 'Sanna' drawn by 16 mules, minus her legs (two wheels) which were drawn by 12 mules. They are not expert liars as they would not have said that the Big Gun has only two wheels; still, a good many Whites and the majority of our people disbelieved our field-glasses in favour of these lies for 'Au Sanna' did not discharge a single shot all day today.

*Tuesday, 19th*

Early this morning we were aroused by the sound of big guns to the west, north, east and south-east. They were the English molesting the Boers, who have heretofore been having things all their own way. The occasional tapping of the Maxims entertained us with that sweet music I have already described, and we enjoyed it advantageously.

The English are amongst the foremost warriors of their day. Here we have only a few soldiers representing the wisdom of their nation in a most demonstrative manner. They not only invent miracles but know how to utilize them at random, under thunder and lightning, through all circumstances.

The large number representing our supply of 'Sanna' for today have only been fired about sunrise in an endeavour to smash up the little English boys, who dare poke their fingers in Big Ben's eye. They are only within a stone's throw of this big gun, but it failed to hit them as not a single Dutchman can see them. They can only see the smoke emanating from the naked ground. The Barolongs who fought Snyman and Cronje, under Montshioa, many years ago, freely admit that if at their time the Boers brought something half the size of 'Sanna' to bear on them, they would have started a mutiny if Montshioa had refused to hoist the white flag after it burst two shells in their village; but today, through the wisdom of the Englishman, 'Sanna' is regarded merely as a member of the Siege community, also entitled to earn a livelihood.

I have not mentioned that when a shell was not well-charged it does not explode when it reaches its destination. People pick them up and sell them; and townsfolk pay for them as follows:

| 1-pounder Maxim Shell | @ | £ | 10–6 |
| The new 5-pounder | @ | £2– | 2–0 |
| A 7-pounder | @ | £ | 15–0 |
| Au Sanna | @ | £6– | 6–0 |

Prices are on the ascent as shells are becoming rare. ('Sanna' formerly sold at £3–0–0.) Yet even if 'Sanna' does explode people do get money for her fragments. The base only fetches 10/6d and the numerous fragments may bring the total for one explosion up to two guineas. These shells are therefore a boon in one sense.

*Wednesday, 20th*

Monday was the hottest day we have had since the Siege, but yesterday was the worst. The heat was intense. Mrs Molema had to clear to the hut for the night with the children, as the house was becoming an oven.[59] I tried to stay and fight it out but was compelled to leave the house to sleep outside at about 11 p.m. I went to sleep in the lee of the house, which I found was as convenient as a garden in the afternoon. I slept soundly until woken by a chilly breeze at 1 a.m. – a marvel of a change for two hours, surely. I felt quite seedy the moment I packed up to turn in again. I knew that it had done me a lot of harm for I had a dazy light head at the time, which caused me to feel very uncomfortable – as I have never felt any sort of pain during the Siege. In the morning I was not able to get up, and I was in bed all day.

Early this morning someone came to tell us that Meko's pretty little daughter had breathed her last and so did old Setuki, an important personage among the Lekomas.[60]

Mausering very mild. Our big guns startled the Boers this morning but the latter made no response. They went for them again this afternoon and a few shots were exchanged. Since Dingaan's Day,[61] Big Ben has had so much to do directly under his nose, that he has had no time to be firing at the homes of women and children and sick people.

*Thursday, 21st*

I have not been able to turn out. I hear that a thief has been sentenced to death today by the Court of Summary Jurisdiction. The C.S.O.[62] will of course have to review the case before the sentence is executed.

At 6 p.m. 'Sanna' discharged a sharp shell which burst in town with extraordinary force. I hear it has once more gone for the ruins of the Mafeking Hotel. I wonder what Mr Riesle did to those Boers?

We feel the strain very much. It is seventeen days since last we had news. If things go on in this way I wonder what our lot is going to be.

*Friday, 22nd*

A quiet morning. Not yet able to get up. It is influenza that I have got.

I hear that two Bangwaketse have been out to loot. They managed to lift some sheep in their choice selection but when they were nearly across the Boer lines during the smaller hours of the morning, one of these sheep commenced to bleat. This put two Boers on their track. What a pity that the two Bangwaketse were not armed as the Boers would presumably not have dreamt to venture near them. The Boers fired several shots at them but with the extraordinary tenacity of the Bechuana in all matters where stock is concerned, one of them preferred to stay with their treasure when the other ran away. The latter came 'to tell the tale'. He says his mate is either killed, caught or wounded. The former is the most probable of the three as they fired very vehemently after our informant took to his heels.

David is really 'wa limala'.[63] Last week he was riding Mr Molema's stallion and it tripped and fell, and both horse and rider were wounded. When he got up with his right side all bruised, he found that the saddle had been neatly placed to the east of him, with the girth cut to pieces; the horse was standing a little to the west bleeding on the knee and forehead. This afternoon he rode to town on my pony – one of the best riding horses in the place. He only got as far as the Railway line when the pony tripped and chucked him over his shoulders and a serious accident took place. His left side (the one that escaped in the stallion incident) and that of the horse, were injured. The bit of my new bridle got twisted 'uit de fatsoen',[64] and [there were] other wrongs and injuries.

I am inclined to attribute it to reckless inattention rather than 'bad luck' as he calls it, for the first time he returned just at the brink of the grave through a similar mishap, and two falls from the best chargers in the country within a week beats creation. Besides we have not been sitting still, and why did we not knock blood out of ourselves and horses, sides, faces, knees, jaws and do other damage [like he did]?

### Saturday, 23rd

An official publication announced that tomorrow will be our Christmas as we cannot depend on the enemy giving us holiday on Monday. So this is our Christmas Eve. A lovely morning, fair and cloudy, giving us a quiet and enjoyable atmosphere. Best of all we have received news after 19 days. It is a lot of news – by private people who of course inform us of the doings of our enemy around us, and bring gossip from the enemy's camp (where newspapers and letters arrive as regularly as ever) – about the occurrences and progress of the war all round the Transvaal, of very recent dates.[65]

### Sunday, 24th

Christmas Day. I am not yet able to turn out but I hear that a good many people are going to keep it up as high as [is] practicable.

I remember my low state with an afflicted sense. To think that this is the second Christmas of my wedded life and I have to spend it, like the first one, so very very far away from the one I love above all: it is becoming too big and I wish I could drive the thought from my mind. Still, I remember last year when I spent three lengthy, solitary days in old Ma-Diamond's [66] beautiful garden and she fed me with the first issues of her fructirous grove in fruits and greeneries. I told her how happy we would both be if my kind little wife, whom she very much longed to see, was with us; we were consoled, however, by the knowledge that she was on that day presenting my first-born to his Saviour under a magnificent Christmas Tree somewhere, and that she would sooner or later bring us our little darling boy who would positively be the happiness of our hearts next Christmas (today), in the same garden, the cultivation of our aged lady friend. But here I am today so very far from having that expectation of our calming meditations fulfilled. I am not even graced with as little as a congratulatory missive from both of them, but am nailed to a sick bed with very poor attention – worst of all, surrounded by Boers. I had expected a ready dressed chicken from my friend Meko as I have developed a dire hatred for all other food, and (indeed) was almost starving when David came from him with two. Hence I discovered that despite my mental tribulations I was not absolutely friendless. I sent back to them St Leger's cream coloured lappie [67] and 'seo sa ga buti'[68] for their little boy, for which they returned hearty Christmas thanks.

I saw little of the open air but all that reached my ears was full of merriment so there must have been some happy things going on.[69] It was raining somewhat pleasantly all the evening.

*Monday, 25th*

A really lovely morning after last night's rain. I went to sit on the verandah and drank deeply of the soft balmy air and enjoyed the atmosphere with the sentiments of one watching a classical show of myth and melody. I only thought – but scarely spoke: everything had brightened up in the most unusual gaiety. Surely we have never had anything like this since the beginning of October; in fact Mafeking never looked so serene all the time I [have] numbered among her inhabitants – and yet I saw Mafeking only as much as was exposed to the eye from the verandah of our house. I have always maintained that no day that the Good Lord will give us during the Siege can in any way equal the ordinary Sunday in beauty – but this excels anything I have yet experienced. I believe that our respected Commander, though mindful of the fact that prudence can never be a mistake, sees that there was no occasion to celebrate the Messiah's nativity yesterday instead of on this most beautiful of glorious days.[70] Pretty well-dressed young men roaming up and down the village and happy voices of hundreds of merry girls to the east and to the west made me wish I was able to rise and admire the proceedings.

Lady Sarah Wilson sent down a collection of toys and sweets for distribution amongst the children of our village. Contented little black faces musing over their gifts reminded me of a little fellow far away, who enjoys whatever he gets at the expense of the comfort of a bewildered young mother, deserving a Christmas box from his father but unable to get it. It squeezed out of my eyes a bitter tear – its course is bitter for I have never felt anything like it since the long and awful nights in 1897 when my path to the union that brought about his birth was so rocky.

Surely Providence has seldom been so hard on me.

### Tuesday, 26th

Early this morning we were aroused by the sound of big guns, muskets and Maxims towards Game Tree. It lasted for nearly an hour, then all was quiet again. It was a good number of the garrison endeavouring to capture a Dutch fort at Game Tree. FitzClarence figured among the ringleaders again and everyone was sure that – bullets failing – he would capture the Dutch fort at the point of the bayonet, but they unfortunately found it a tough business. They got up to the fort and were preparing to jump right into it amongst the Boers. But the walls were so high that only a few managed to get on top. Even here they could do nothing as the trench was too well roofed and the Boers, who meanwhile had their rifles through the loopholes, played havoc with them until they hoisted the Red Cross. FitzClarence alone got inside and stabbed two or three. They shot him once but he proceeded to bayonet another when they shot a second time and he dropped down – though not dead. (Three who went to the door of the trench were taken prisoners.) He is now in the hospital improving. I think [that] the wounding of FitzClarence incapacitates an eminent 'moguli'[71] from taking part in future operations against the Transvaal, when the Troops cross the border. The Boers never hit so hard a blow on Mafeking since they besieged us. Altogether we lost 23 men killed and 26 wounded. The rest of the day was quiet.[72]

### Wednesday, 27th

A very quiet and pleasant day, fair and cloudy. I was able to get up this morning and hope to be about soon. Nothing happened during the day. In the evening David entertained me with some Lenkoaniacs,[73] which I enjoyed very much. He once found Hyena Jones covered with a thick blanket in his room in the daytime. David's lips were just about to part when he hushed him in a faint voice and informed him that his time was extremely short – so short that the devil already knew with how many nitches of the tape-measure it will 'lingaana'.[74] I presume it is to be inferred from this that Jones' soul will go to the devil when it departs this life. David, however, took to himself the liberty of putting to him certain abridged interrogations concerning his ailment in the most sympathetic manner, and to his surprise every one of his queries made Hyena 'weller'.[75] He was travelling so accurately though slowly along the path of recovery that he was eventually able to remove the thick blanket off his body with the extraordinary remark that his respect for David was as great as his astonishment at his piousness. For David was among the very rare specimens of Christianity on the face of the globe able to cure a dying person simply by motion of their lips; and he stood up and started tidying the room with his usual healthy and civilised way of doing things. Besides a lot more he [David] told me how Hyena once determined to settle the love question with his rival with a thing a little more deadly than his tongue – for which purpose he procured a rifle. He took a companion with him and bragged as they went along – but he forgot to shoulder the rifle, and took to his heels immediately the rival put in an appearance. On one occasion (shortly after his arrival) Jones nearly assaulted him for having told an enquirer that Mrs Lenkoane was at work, instead of which she had gone out for a walk – he told some such lie. 'Mma, ke tseba bora ba batho ba jwale ka bo Phooko. When ach yue khoing to atopt the wase of sophilised people. Ke sa tsua chata hona jwale. What will the chentleman think of me to hear that my wife is at work.' [76]

Our Civil Commissioner is a white Lenkoane. His acumen in fixing sarcastic phrases and aptitude in putting comical jokes is beyond description. His mere silence gives him a very ferocious appearance.

On Sunday he sent word to all hands that his servants – he had about a dozen of them – should all turn up on Monday to a grand Christmas dinner he was going to give them. They rolled up en masse, but were surprised to find everything in much the same manner as when the pudding party in no.III Royal Reader got some pudding [77] – except that these poor fellows received not even the aroma of a grand Christmas dinner. The Officers came for their meal at the usual hour, and when they departed the ole buck [78] quickly retired to his bomb-proof for his after-lunch siesta – leaving the disappointed menials to take their way, with dismay written on their faces in bold letters. This is Wednesday already, and he has not yet offered them the slightest excuse for the inopportune treatment.

### Thursday, 28th

It is raining very much. Two runners came in from the south this morning. Everybody is full to overflowing, the news they brought being too sweet and too much for the capacity of the human stomach. They bring news of two victories by our Relief Party – one at 14 Streams [79] and one at Phokwane. The former was on the 18th. As Lady Sarah Wilson came here on the 7th and heard in the Boer Laar that Lord Methuen had arrived in Kimberley, we have expected this for a very long time.

I am afraid someone's stomach will burst – so nice is the news. Mr

Molema last night brought me a copy of the *Bulawayo Chronicle*, from Captain Marsh. It was dated the 2nd Instant, a very early date for any newspaper. Every paper, unfortunate enough to find its way into Kimberley, must pass through so many hands, that when one comes across it it is quite worn out and requires to be handled with the greatest care. It contained two accounts of Lord Methuen's fighting at Belmont [80] against Free State Burghers. One account was the Dutch General's reports to Oom Paul [81] on the same fight, reproduced from the Standard and Diggers News. The other was the British report, on the same affair received by an official dispatch from Cape Town.

*Report No. I* says: I had a heavy fight all day against the British troops under General Buller and killed no fewer than two thousand (2,000) of them; commandant Some-one-or-other was wounded in the arm but not before he inflicted serious losses on them. The Burghers stuck to their ground well, but were compelled to retreat by the overwhelming number of the English who covered five miles of ground. There were 7,000 of them against 1,400 Burghers. They had 24 cannons and we had only 4.

It is impossible to give the number of our losses. Still it is not great.

*Report No. II* was pert and pithy: we drove them from one kopje [82] to the other in each of which they had strong fortification. From the last we repulsed them with 4 guns posted on the opposite kopje and they retired so hurriedly they did not stop to take shelter in the Laager. We destroyed the Laager, 50,000 rounds of rifle ammunition and 300 shells. Altogether we took 40 prisoners and buried 20 dead Boers. We lost 58 Officers and men killed, and 151 wounded.

I suppose the local General reported on Tuesday about Game Tree that he fought the whole of Mafeking Garrison with a stray scrap of his commando and killed 600 British – half of the Garrison. This discrepancy is something like a report of the fight on the Natal side of the border, in which a Boer Commandant infuriated by the British, says there were 10,000 British troops against 800 Boers, only 400 of whom were fighting.[83]

### Friday, 29th

The rain stopped for a while last night and started again this morning. It continued all day today. Mausering was consequently very mild. Only 'Sanna' went very hot today.

I was able to turn out this morning and found many people in town down with the sickness I had – it's influenza. I returned from town just in time, for the rains started two minutes before I reached home. I did some interpreting for half the Dutch womenfolk of the Women's Laager

in a very long case in court. It was the only one, but kept me busy for a
longer period than the usual session when ten or fourteen cases are on
the roll. It was a charge against a Dutch damsel, a member of a local
well-known family, of having stolen £90—12—0, the property of a lady
of the same nationality. Both complainant and accused are domiciled
in the Women's Laager and the former carried this money about her, as
it would have been commandeered if she took it to the Standard Bank.[84]
The mode of living in the Women's Laager is so shabby that there was
no safer place for the money than her handbag, and that is how the
unfortunate girl got access to it. They are a family of 'mahlwembu'[85]
who had severally been under pecuniary embarrassments. Her lavish
purchases and repeated acts of generosity laid the robbery bare. The
prisoner pleaded not guilty. The case is remanded till tomorrow —
Saturday the 30th.

The Game Tree fiasco appears to have been a heartrending burlesque.
Never was such a wilful suicide committed by a community in our condition. The Colonel commanding — it appears — was forced into permission of the thing against his will. He recently wanted the Barolong
to go and capture the cattle from the Western Boer Laar. But Lekoko [86]
gave him such reasonable reasons that he convinced him to the belief
that everyone would be killed before seeing the cattle, and all the heart
in him dwindled away; he [87] was bound to believe that the greatest and
most prominent way of proving our bravery would be by sitting quietly
and defending our place until the arrival of the Troops.[88]

He [89] also went half way with them and at dawn they advanced towards the place, walking along in broad daylight, the Boers having their
rifles cocked through the loopholes just waiting for them to approach.
It is a marvellous thing that they were not all killed, for it was a regular
self-murder, as they had no cover whatever. The Boers waited until
they were within a hundred yards — then loosed a hail of bullets among
them. The officers took the lead and skipped towards the 'armoured
trench' — every one of the men following. They jumped on top with the
intention of using the bayonets, but found the place too well roofed
for the purpose. The Boers were meanwhile playing havoc with the
others who were then endeavouring to shoot them through their own
loop-holes. They were already without officers when they reached the
fort. Some had revolvers even through the loop-holes, and one held
the barrel of a Mauser on the outside and stuck his bayonet past it. It
was a lamentable affair and the least said about it the better. The
consternation amongst the inhabitants was so deeply rooted that it is
clearly visible amongst men and women and old and young of both
whites and blacks.

*Saturday, 30th*

A West African, giving evidence in a city police court, once described the cause of the proceedings as 'a h-ll of a smash', but I believe a real 'h-ll of a smash' was the wreck of the Charge Office by 'Sanna' this morn. Such a destruction of the Charge Office is really a narrow shave for the Court House. Many or all of the prominent places like Whiteley's, Weil's, Dixon's, the Bank, the neat little rondavel of the Market Hut, etc. have all taken their turns in the test of 'Sanna's' dexterity, but the Court House, much to the extreme disgust of the inhabitants who, seeing Sanna's agility at wrecking buildings, imagined that, it being the head official building, it was their chance of getting the new Court they have so long been agitating for. I believe it's saved intentionally by the Boers, for the Residency also, and the Gaol, have never been hit. Turning to our subject, the ruin of the Charge Office was just as lamentable as many of 'Sanna's' doings, and it was also the occasion of a marvellous escapade. It entered, and shook down the office. It found 50 Natives, who had taken shelter in front of the ill-fated building when the Toesins [90] chimed. The many fragments found their way away from the presence of human beings and only singled out a good young fellow (one of the Maseloas), threw the top of his head away from his body, and left him standing exactly where he was: all this was the work of a second – or a lesser period. Every one of his companions spent a long time reflecting over the narrowness of his own escape. Sheets, half sheets and fragments of corrugated iron were scattered all over the street, and they did not notice the occurrence till many minutes after.

A deserted young Zulu from the Boers reports that at the unfortunate burlesque, the fiasco at Game Tree on Tuesday morning, 10 Boers were killed, and 10 wounded. They say it was Jameson who attacked them.[91] Miss Bezuidenhout's case [92] has not yet been decided: it is further remanded until Tuesday.

Young Maseloa was buried in their kraal today.

*Sunday, 31st*

Ou-Jaarsdag.[93] The usual thing. No thunder and no danger. The Colonel and Civil Commissioner were down to settle an issue amongst the Chiefs. The cause of the trouble was of course – Thelesho.[94]

With Sidzumo, Nyanzi and Miss Moloza, in the afternoon I went to have a close scrutiny of my Dutch friends across the disputed territory.

We called in at 7 p.m. He [95] was halfway at his cups and had a great many objections to make. He wondered why the Authorities, seeing that the whites are afraid of the Boers, don't arm the Barolong, as they would certainly go and rifle the 'God-damned brutes away'. And also, why the issue of grain has since this morning been so regulated that no-one is allowed to buy more than 6*d* worth at a time.

The former [96] would cause us to run over to the enemy and ask him for permission to settle outside peacefully and plough as usual, while the latter would evoke such a mutiny in camp as would put an end to the Siege – which wouldn't be existing at the end of next week. He also set us giggling by informing us how Wessels habitually parts with his £50 after receiving his quarterly allowance: he would send several Cape Boys to buy some brandy for him. He would keep on sending one after the other and the last two or three would depart when the first had already returned, after which the old fellah would be so miserably under the exuberance of the damning drink as not to recognise the rest of them. Each of them would then pocket the 3/- and not bother about buying the Brandy at all.

The process would be just the same with others whose role it was to visit the Butcher, Baker, Grocer etc. The messages would be duplicated, triplicated and even quadruplicated, and as the necessary money would be furnished on each occasion, they would all stand by quietly and wait for the first Cape Boy, then safely convert the money to their own use, without fear of any judicial proceedings.

EDITORIAL NOTE

The nature of the siege changed unmistakably in December, and this month set the tone for things to come. The Boers did not attack during the period, though rumour had it that one offensive was cancelled at the last moment. Thus, apart from the Game Tree incident, confrontation was restricted to artillery bombardment, sniping and brief skirmishes.

The two internal enemies faced by the besieged populace, however, began to make themselves felt: accidents through the detonation of unexploded shells accounted for life and limb, and boredom became a creeping paralysis that demanded an antidote. Diversionary activity, aimed at distracting and amusing the citizenry of Mafeking, was planned in an attempt to alleviate this primary discomfort. Sundays saw the organisation of gymkanas, polo matches and other sports in which the military and civilian populations participated enthusiastically. Baden-Powell himself played a leading role: apart from playing polo, he arranged satirical pageantry – in which he appeared as a ludicrously overdressed ringmaster – in order to boost morale. The *Mafeking Mail* also injected a measure of fun into this by printing results and, more often than not, lively comment. Also, Sunday-night concerts were presented. A music ensemble entertained audiences with more serious items while Baden-Powell and any others who could be recruited provided musical and satirical sketches. This revelry – which depended for its success on Boer recognition of the Sunday truce – no doubt relieved the pressure on the besieged population. Perhaps this is one reason why the Africans of *Mafikeng*, who had little part in the diversionary activities, were later to feel the pressure to a far greater extent than their allies across the railway line.

Although these programmes broke the monotony with weekly regularity, Christmas was a singular occasion. The townsfolk – with the energetic help of Ben Weil – ate festive dinners, either at the hotels (which provided surprisingly sumptuous repasts, when it is considered that rationing was soon to be imposed) or in shell-damaged homes. Morale was high – especially as a result of the 'double' Christmas brought about by the unique situation. But this was to ebb the very next day with the Game Tree disaster.

On the Boer side of the line of investment a general 'tightening-up' was being put into effect. Hence, while little attempt was made to enter the town, they made quite sure that it would be equally difficult to leave it. Their success is measured by the fact that cattle-raiders, dispatch-runners and spies found it increasingly difficult to pass through the Boer lines. One might have expected that Baden-Powell's proclamation of 10 December would have been followed by an escalation in their offensive; but this never occurred. Instead the Boers sat tight and permitted the hardships of the besieged to take their course. In fact, few physical difficulties had yet been faced. In town there was still an adequate supply of food, and the citizenry were becoming accustomed to the regular explosion of shells. The picture in the *stadt*, where shelling accounted for more lives, was not quite as optimistic – yet it was far from serious. True, grazing had become scarce (although frequent rains ameliorated this situation too). But the Barolong were still far from eating the dog-flesh that became a substantial part of their diet later on.

CHAPTER NOTES

1 Kuruman, the site of much of Robert Moffat's mission work among the Batlharo, is approximately 190 miles from Mafeking. It lies in a south-westerly direction.

2 The *Vierkleur* (Dutch: literally, 'four colour') was the flag of the Transvaal Republic. It had a vertical green stripe, and horizontal orange, white and blue stripes.

3 This is a Barolong boo Ratlou village in the Vryburg district.

4 Letlhogile was chief of the Mariba branch of the Barolong boo Ratlou tribe of Ganyesa. The Ratlou are not to be confused with the Barolong boo Rapulana who allied themselves with the Boers.

5 The actual word written in the text is indecipherable and the editor has taken

the liberty of introducing 'Au Sanna', as this was clearly the diarist's intended meaning.

6 The relevant report in the *Mafeking Mail* of 1 December reads as follows: 'The Boers had two pieces of artillery knocked out by us at the Waterworks affair on October 23rd.' The battle alluded to was one fought solely between the artillerists, and there had been considerable speculation as to its real outcome before this report arrived.

7 This is an understatement of the size of the garrison (see Prologue, p. 30).

8 Dutch: 'patch of ground'. Again Plaatje chooses to use a Dutch word, and again it does not appear to be an arbitrary choice. The area concerned was interstitial and dangerous; to stray into it was to move into the realm of Boer control. The diarist's use of Dutch reflects this – the correlation between the introduction of another language and its sociological relevance is too frequent to be arbitrary.

9 Mr H. Whiteley was the Mayor of Mafeking before and during the siege.

10 Many such false reports arrived in Mafeking. Kimberley was only relieved on 15 February, and the first reliable report reached Mafeking in the last week of that month.

11 Tswana: 'greet', 'salute'.

12 Linchwe (or Lentswe) was chief of the Bakgatla tribe at Mochudi in the Bechuanaland Protectorate. Before the war he sent his brother, Segale, to negotiate with the Boers on the basis that although this was a white-man's war, he would resist any attempt to violate his territory. At the same time he promised not to act as aggressor (which he could not have done anyway as he lacked the strength). The Boers, for reasons which have often been hotly debated, overran two Bakgatla villages without facing resistance. Soon after, Lentswe's warriors ambushed an ammunition convoy in the Marico District. With the conquered arms they repulsed what were alleged to be two further invasions (the exact location of these confrontations being unclear), and entered Boer territory. It is to this expedition that Plaatje's entry refers.

13 This usage represents a linguistic mixture: *-azi* or *-kazi* are Nguni feminine suffixes; the *k* (of Nguni) is pronounced as *h* when transposed into Sotho-Tswana. (*k → h* is a regular sound-shift). Hence the word means 'Barolong women'.

14 This is Sotho-Tswana. Exact translation is difficult as the word *fela* (or *hela*) has more than one meaning. In Sotho it is an auxiliary verb that means 'certainly' or 'indeed'. In Tswana it can mean 'everything', 'all' or 'certainly'; as an auxiliary verb it means 'to continue'. Thus in Sotho the sentence may be translated as 'They might indeed (certainly) have killed them.' In Tswana the most appropriate translation would seem to be 'They might have killed them all.'

15 The officer referred to was Gordon Wilson. His wife, Lady Sarah (daughter of the Duke of Marlborough), took refuge at Setlagoli (some fifty miles south-west of Mafeking) at the beginning of the siege. There is a second version of the manner in which she fell into Boer hands. Apparently, after dodging the Boers for some time, she obtained a carrier pigeon, which was intercepted with a message warning the garrison of her impending arrival. As a result – the story goes – she was apprehended and delivered up to Snyman, whose insistence that she be exchanged for Viljoen led to a lengthy correspondence. The place, Mosita, referred to in the same sentence, is approximately twenty miles west of Setlagoli and fifty-five miles west-south-west of Mafeking.

16 *Redan*: 'A fortification with two parapets meeting at a salient angle'.

17 These were the Irish Sisters of Mercy who occupied the convent; they were

removed to safer accommodation when shelling in their vicinity became heavy.

18 *Mafeking Mail*, 6 December. Plaatje has reproduced the article in full.

19 *Go thiba* (Tswana): 'to turn back', 'stop', 'obstruct', etc. The actual word in the text is difficult to decipher, but this seems most possible and comprehensible. The word is also used in Sotho, but its meaning ('stop', 'obstruct', 'prevent', 'impede', etc.) is slightly different. The Sotho-Tswana range of meaning is most apt to describe the operation. Again here Plaatje chooses a Tswana word to describe a sphere of action that, during the siege, belonged to the Africans alone.

20 The Reuter war-correspondent.

21 This is a Tswana verb. It means 'lie down to be beaten' or 'beaten when lying down'. The English suffix *-ing* transposes the sense of the word from verb to gerund. Plaatje's use of the vernacular in an unexpected context (and its juxtaposition with the English suffix *-ing*) succeeds in conveying the humour in a tragic situation.

22 Efforts to trace this reference have proved fruitless.

23 Probably the translation of the Dutch *baster*: 'person of mixed ethnic stock'.

24 Xhosa-Zulu: 'leopard'. Southern Bantu frequently use animal allegory. Here the leopard, as an animal of prey, is a metaphor for the greatest threat to the besieged town – the Creusot siege-gun.

25 This is the phonetic spelling of Viljoen. Lady Sarah's arrival was treated as something of a festive occasion, and her romantic escapades became a talking-point for the news-hungry townspeople.

26 Dutch: 'angry' or 'hot-tempered'.

27 This word definitely appears in the text. It is not clear what meaning is intended.

28 Properly *isinge* (Xhosa). A class 7 noun, it means 'back'.

29 In fact Plaatje omits its completely. However, as it was printed in the *Mafeking Mail* of 11 December, it is reproduced here in full. The fact that he mentions, on 8 December, a communication dated the 10th, indicates that he had fallen behind on his entries. It is possible that on some week-days time did not permit writing and the diary was brought up to date on Sunday.

30 It is reported that Baden-Powell refused at first to consent to the exchange, but that Lord Edward Cecil persuaded him to accept the Boer demand.

31 Plaatje often uses the word 'herd' instead of 'shepherd' or 'herdsman' in the text.

32 Presumably a near-by Boer laager.

33 Dutch: 'straps' or 'thongs'.

34 At the time of the siege Bokone was about a mile from the centre of the *stadt*. In its subsequent growth the village eventually encompassed this area. *Bokone* (Setswana) means 'north'.

35 Xhosa: 'scarce'. By using a non-Tswana word, Plaatje emphasises how prized this loot must have been to the envious non-Tswana men of the 'Black Watch'.

36 When Barolong speak in English, of judicial proceedings, they tend to say 'the case is . . . (for example, adultery)'. This results from the direct translation of Setswana usage. Hence we may guess that Plaatje is trying to say that the case arising out of this incident was one of 'sticking up' (i.e., robbery).

37 Or *Qhuma*. Zulu: 'pop', 'crack' or 'burst'. The click pronunciation of the *q*, suggests onomatopoeia.

38 Used synonymously with 'Kgalagari'. Some Sotho-Tswana consonants, for reasons that are too complex to discuss here, are used interchangeably. This also explains 'Bakgalagalis' in the next sentence but one. Both 'Kalahari' and 'Bakgalagali' are frequently used by contemporary Barolong.

39 Dutch: 'five hundred' and 'ten hundred' respectively. The Dutch is probably used here to emphasise the authenticity of the report – it implies an admission by the Boers. It may also be that 'tien honderd' is preferred to 'a thousand' in order to emphasise that Boer losses were double those of the English.

40 Here he uses the original Barolong name for Mafeking. It is the locative form of the word *mafika* ('rocks').

41 Tau was the last effective ruler of a united Barolong people. He died in about 1760, and it was in the lifetime of his sons that the Barolong divided into four branches. The name Tau means 'Lion'. In fact, the Barolong migrated southwards before 1750, and there is no record of their having lived in Ngamiland. Furthermore, *Mafikeng* was founded – and named – approximately a century after the death of Tau. But this is not simply erroneous history; it reflects one important aspect of the Tshidi-Barolong conscious model of their relations with the Boers.

42 Tswana: literally, 'they who are uplifted and fierce'. The expression, according to one Tshidi informant, implies that they were supernaturally inspired. One point of clarification: the second word of the sentence (*rungwana*: 'lifted up', 'raised', 'uplifted') has a diminutive suffix. This can, and may here, be used to convey affection.

43 A British newspaper for which Angus Hamilton wrote frequently during the siege.

44 Reverend Briscoe was the Methodist missionary in the *stadt*. The mission-house stands opposite the 'Warren' church (built in 1885 by Warren's engineers) across the Molopo. The drift was the point at which the river could be crossed between the church and the mission-house, and must have been close to Plaatje's home.

45 A species of tree common in the district.

46 Tiego was the son of Selere, the younger brother of the late chief Montshiwa. He was a cousin (father's brother's son) of Wessels, the chief during the siege, and later became a prominent man in tribal politics. The 'corps' referred to is the age-regiment of which Tiego was leader. Having been formed in 1892, it was the most recently founded at the time.

47 I.e. the railway line.

48 Plaatje probably did not bother to copy out the Proclamation as it was printed both as a hand-out and as an article in the *Mafeking Mail*. From his mention of the 'accompanying circular', we may guess that the diarist slipped a copy into his notebook, and that this was lost. It is therefore reproduced here in full.

49 The Zuid-Afrikaansche Republiek, established after the first Boer War (1880). Paul Kruger became its president in 1883.

50 This dispatch also carried an angry retort from Snyman. The *Mafeking Mail* (13 December) reports the communication as follows: 'General Snyman has written with regard to Colonel Baden-Powell's circular addressed to the Burghers. He is very incensed at its having been sent direct to them, and is apparently much annoyed at the remark that "sitting down and looking at a place is not the way to take it". He challenges us to come out and drive them away. He also explains that, far from the Burghers being kept in the dark by their commanders and newspapers, the opposite is the case. . . .'

51 Lord Methuen, a former Governor of Natal, was appointed Commander of the First Division Army Corps when the war broke out. A successful soldier in many African campaigns, he was heavily defeated at Magersfontein on 11 December. The news that the British Army had lost over 1,000 men in this battle had not yet reached Mafeking.

52 In the manuscript this word is spelt *uninikazi*. However, it is almost certain

that Plaatje intended *uninakazi*. This is a Zulu kinship term, and means 'his mother's sister (maternal aunt)'. It is obviously used to specify the relationship between Sibale and Mrs Sidzumo. From the fact that the family concerned lived in the 'location', we may guess that they were of Nguni (or, at least, non-Tswana) origin. This may explain Plaatje's choice of a non-Tswana term,

53 I.e., back from the *stadt* to the house in the location.

54 Plaatje implies here that most of their news was secured by Barolong spies.

55 *Mafeking Mail*, 18 December.

56 The last three paragraphs show evidence of multiple alteration. The editor has taken the liberty of reproducing the most coherent version possible. The 'old General' was obviously Joubert.

57 As there is no other reference to this item, it has been impossible to identify the person or source concerned. The incident is unrelated to the one described in the next paragraph.

58 *Hamba* (Xhosa) and *inkomo* (Zulu) mean 'go' and 'head of cattle' respectively. The combination is intended to mean 'to move cattle' – i.e., to raid. It is a clumsy usage; for the sake of exactitude, if nothing else, the verb should be written as a causative (*hambisa*). Plaatje, who is usually fastidious in his Bantu usage, may be using linguistic clumsiness to reflect the clumsiness of the operation. While this interpretation may appear to flatter the diarist, comparison with his use of language to reflect behaviour in other contexts makes this explanation possible. The use of Zulu suggests that the men concerned were non-Tswana living in the location. (Had they been members of the Black Watch special mention would probably have been made.)

59 Barolong families that could command the necessary resources tended to build European-style homesteads. These generally had a few outhouses built in the manner of traditional huts.

60 The Lekomas were at the time, and are still, a large and influential Tshidi-Barolong family group.

61 Celebrated on 16 December, this is the anniversary of the defeat of 10,000 of Dingaan's Zulus by a party of Boer trekkers at the battle of Blood River in Natal, in 1838.

62 The acting Chief Staff Officer at this time was Major Panzera, who also commanded the artillery. The permanent C.S.O. was Lord Edward Cecil.

63 This should be written as one word (*walimala*). Being Xhosa-Zulu, it is in the stative and means 'he was injured (hurt, crippled, etc.)'.

64 Dutch: 'out of shape'. In a footnote Plaatje adds that the bridle subsequently broke.

65 This and half of the next entry are again written in the second handwriting alluded to earlier. The fact that Plaatje was at this time laid up with influenza adds weight to the opinion that these passages were dictated by him to an unknown scribe. Here, as in the previous case, spelling and punctuation degenerate, words are omitted, and careless errors abound. Immediately on the resumption of Plaatje's own script, these shortcomings are eliminated. (See footnotes to the entry of 24 November.)

66 Mrs Diamond. There is no way of expressing 'Mrs' in Tswana. A married woman is referred to by the prefix *Mma* (literally 'mother'), followed by her husband's or son's name. It has proved impossible to trace the woman referred to.

67 Dutch: 'a small rag, or cloth'. It is probable that he intended some item of clothing.

68 Tswana: 'the thing (unspecified) that belongs to my elder brother'. *Bhuti*, translated here as 'elder brother', is not actually Tswana. It is a Nguni

corruption of the Dutch *boetie* (brother) that is sometimes heard among Barolong. It has been pointed out to me that this phrase may be a euphemism for something of which direct mention is avoided.

69  The Christmas celebrations were indeed elaborate. Lady Sarah Wilson and Ben Weil organised a tea-party, complete with decorated tree, for some 250 children of the town. Sports were arranged for the adults in the afternoon. Judging from the reports of lavish dinners, the atmosphere in town appears to have belied its besieged state. There are no reports of celebrations in the *stadt*, but it would seem that the Barolong had to rely on spiritual rather than culinary satisfaction.

70  Baden-Powell 'rescheduled' Christmas because of his belief that the Boers celebrate New Year rather than this holy day. In fact, there were no hostilities from either side on the 25th.

71  Or *mogodi*. Tswana: 'a leader', 'distinguished one'. Plaatje may have intended a pun here, for *godi* means 'gunpowder' (the *mo-* in this context being the class-one subjectival concord implying a person).

72  Several reasons have been advanced for Baden-Powell's decision to attack Game Tree, a Boer fort to the north-east of the town. Among them, the need for more pasturage, for a morale-booster, and for retaining some initiative are the three most quoted. But secondary reasons – the neutralisation of the point from which the convent, hospital and the Women's Laager was being shelled and the opening of a way for the relief column – have also been suggested.

The Boers got wind of the impending attack and strengthened their fortifications to good effect. Two squadrons of the Protectorate Regiment, under captains FitzClarence and Vernon (who was killed) advanced, with support from the armoured train and artillery. They met heavy fire and registered more losses than in any other confrontation. The final casualty-list included 24 killed, 23 wounded, and 3 captured. (Plaatje's figures are more accurate than any other siege diarists' here.)

73  Stories about Lenkoane. Evidently 'Hyena Jones' was Lenkoane's nickname.

74  Zulu-Xhosa; properly spelt *'lingana'*, it means 'to be equal to'. It has been suggested to me that the reference here is to time; the devil knows the exact measurement of his remaining time by measuring it against a tape.

75  I.e., 'better'.

76  'Mma, ke tseba . . . my wife is at work.' The four sentences are, with the exception of the Tswana auxiliary verb *mma* ('look here', 'wait a minute'), mainly a mixture of Southern Sotho and Hyena's Sotho-accented English. The first sentence means 'Look here, I know the enmity of people such as Phooko' (the person who enquired about Mrs Lenkoana). The second sentence ('When are you going to adopt the ways of civilised people') is a representation of Sotho-accented English. Its accuracy is, I am told, remarkable – especially in regard to the emphasis of consonants. The third sentence – with the exception of *chata* (Xhosa: 'marry') – is again Southern Sotho, and means 'I have just now (got) married.' The fourth sentence is clear, with only the g- (gentleman) being replaced by ch-.

The story of Hyena Jones, the comic, is a playful satire characterised by linguistic imitation. Plaatje recounts with obvious mirth Hyena's exaggerated claim to be dying, and his remarkable recovery brought about by David's questions. The bragging and the cowardice with which Hyena intended to settle the 'love question' is juxtaposed with his hurt ('On one occasion . . . at work') at the fact that people like Phooko would gossip about his wife earning money for him. Hyena is the personification of a human foible: he moralises about the undesirability of men being supported by their wives – and lies in order to deny that he is such a man. The sentence 'When ach yue . . . sophilised people' is puzzling, as it appears to be addressed to David; it is possible, however, that *yue* is simply Hyena's clumsy English and that he intended *they*. Alternatively, Hyena might have been referring to the 'enquirer'.

77 The allusion here is to one of the books from which Plaatje learned English. This English reader was used in most South African (African) schools at the turn of the century.

78 Mr Bell, the Civil Commissioner.

79 A village on the Vaal River on the Cape–Transvaal border.

80 Belmont lies approximately fifty-five miles south of Kimberley.

81 President Kruger of the Transvaal.

82 Dutch: 'hillock'.

83 The latter half of the entry for 28 December and the first paragraph of that of the 29th are again written in the second handwriting. As explained earlier, the necessary corrections have been made.

84 The only bank in town at the time. When shelling became heavy, it was transferred to an underground shelter and operated from there.

85 Properly *amahlwempu* (sing. *ihlwempu*). Xhosa: 'the needy people'.

86 Lekoko was a cousin (father's brother's son) of chief Wessels. Due to the fact that he was an older man of considerable political influence among the Tshidi, and the acting chief was both weak and uninterested in public affairs, Lekoko was the effective tribal leader during the siege.

87 It is not clear whether he is referring to Baden-Powell or to Lekoko.

88 This is an interesting aside on the attack which is not documented elsewhere. That Plaatje had access to it is quite possible, for he spent much time in the company of the most senior of Baden-Powell's staff. This remark is most relevant in assessing both the propriety of the decision to attack the fort, and the real reasons for it. (See footnote 72 above.) One obvious possibility that has not been considered is the eagerness of the garrison to 'have a go' at the Boers. We know that pressure of this sort was brought to bear on Baden-Powell later on in the siege. More attention should perhaps be paid to its relevance on this occasion.

89 Baden-Powell; he took up his position at Fort Dummy, which lay between the town and Game Tree.

90 Dutch: 'take care', 'be warned'. This refers to the warning bell. (See also the entry of 16 February.)

91 Jameson had been in Mafeking just prior to the siege, but left before hostilities began. Perhaps this reference to Jameson was jocular: he had been defeated easily before, why not again?

92 The case of theft in the Women's Laager, mentioned above.

93 Dutch: 'old-year's day'.

94 Thelesho was the fifth son of Molema, the founder of *Mafikeng*. The family group of which he was a member frequently acted as a faction in opposition to the ruling descendants of Montshiwa and their political supporters. Thelesho was, until his death some years later, a very active tribal politician. The issue referred to is too involved to report here: it concerned Chief Wessel's alleged mismanagement of Tshidi tribal affairs.

95 It is not clear who is meant by 'he' in this case. It is obviously the same person referred to in the second sentence of the following paragraph, but there is no clue as to his identity.

96 The use of 'former' and 'latter' here is confusing; both would seem to relate more appropriately to the grain issue than to any other mentioned.

# 3   January 1900

*Monday, 1st*

The first day of the first week of the first month in 1900. Not at all a lovely morning. The distant pop of the Mauser distinctly shows that there is no holiday for poor beleaguered us. I tried to go to town but 'Au Sanna', going strong, caused me to come back and take shelter. I wonder why some people call her 'Grietje', as 'Griet'[1] for a thing of her potency, would be nearer the mark. She was exceptionally 'kwaai' all day today. Goodness knows what provoked her.

After I went to town and David and Ebie[2] were breaking-fast the thing smashed within 50 yards from the house. David cleared helter-skelter with the coffee which had become insipid. Ebie considered his bread too precious and remained chewing as if nothing had happened. In the afternoon things were very warm. I have developed a nasty fear for 'Sanna'. She has, since Dingaan's Day, devoted her time to our little gun across the river, and we have now become unused to her. I wonder why she is so hot today.

In the afternoon David stood watching a train of merry girls, amidst whom were Meko's sisters-in-law in the best of millineries, celebrating the New Year with several jolly games. All of a sudden 'Sanna' came round and spoiled the whole thing. Mr Briscoe's garden is an intolerably near spot for 94 pounds of mortar to burst while a train of giggling girls are enjoying the first day in the first year of the twentieth century near Bokone – particularly when they were under the impression that it was directed to town. It sent nearly all the merry maidens in different directions. Some lay flat on the ground – it was for dear life – and 'Sanna' fairly put them in memory that their lives were dearer and more expensive than their New Year's dresses. One shell burst near Weil's this morning. The employers had a narrow escape and two mules which happened to be about were killed on the spot. One burst near the Commissariat yard. A fragment came in contact with one of the labourers and eviscerated him which, in short, means killed him on the spot. A few broken walls completed the total for today. 'Sanna' was very hot today, and so was a beastly new seven-pounder to the east of

the town which at one time caused me to leave the Market Square
post haste – it was for dear life.

## Tuesday, 2nd

The 7-pounder that fired from the east yesterday had been moved
round to Jackal Tree during the night. It sent a number of shells into the
Stadt early this morning, one of which smashed inside the hut of Mma-
Mokoloi and emptied its contents on her head. None of the others were
injured. The baby at her breast was not even shaken. A shell from
'Sanna' hit the east of the Stadt, where Ellitson has put up his slaughter-
pole since the Siege,[3] and amputated an employee in a most pitious
manner – both legs and both arms. He died after this.

## Wednesday, 3rd

It was not the seven-pounders which killed Rra-Mokoloi's wife, but
a twelve-pounder. Opinions differ on the point and some call it nine-
pounder, however its shells are said to be far more dangerous than any
yet used by the enemy on Mafeking. It is posted somewhere west of the
Stadt.

They have turned their attention away from the Rooi-neks[4] and
have decided to knock spots out of the verdomde[5] Kaffers this morning. They are shelling the Stadt from east and west. There is a miscellaneous collection of Natives from Johannesburg who thought that the
war would last but a month or less. They came here as they thought
Mafeking was safe enough to spend the month, after which they would
return to the revolutionised Rand. They are a miscellaneous collection
and include Pondos, Shangaans, Barotse, Zambesian and South Central
African breeds. They are a harmless lot of people – some of them live
under the two trees on the space between the B.S.A. Police Camp and
the Stadt. They do a little night's toil when they require a little cash
to buy grain which they 'nona'[6] with horseflesh. They are quiet and are
waiting for the end of this trouble, and I am sure they would not do any
harm to anybody. This morning I was trying to go to town. I was just
near the two trees when the bells rang. There was a horrible smash all
round me and I could see the branches of one of the trees flying in the
air in a cloud of dust. From under the tree all the men in the shade were
raised from 4 to 7 foot high. After the smash I thought that thunder
seldom strikes twice the same place, and I pressed my nerves to see how
my fellow creatures had been jumped upon by this meanest part of the
scum of the German race. But the Good Lord's potency is marvellously
demonstrative when he wishes to frustrate the termination of a wicked
man. His good angels had preceded the shell, shifted the men apart,
and made a way for it. It burst amongst them in a most indescribable

awfulness, but not one of them was hurt. There was a furrow where it ploughed the ground among their bedding. The Camelthorn tree suffered fearfully, but not one of the men got a single scratch. However I was filled with fear and I turned back to take shelter. I had hardly reached the Meko's when there was another terrific smash. It burst five yards from them; this time the fragment flew over their heads but injured nobody. Things were a bit quiet about dinner time. The 12-pounder was meanwhile circuiting back to the East. It took up its position, apparently to resume operations in the afternoon, but they had hardly time to digest their lunch of black coffee and ox meat when Baden-Powell's chappies showed them that they had something nasty for Boer flesh in store in Mafeking. Three 7-pounders, posted within range of the big gun last night, and a little Nordenfeld started to boom one by one. Their shells raised clouds of dust as they demolished the earth-works which form the Boer's entrenchments. The little Nordenfeld is a very great friend of 'Sanna's' — we'll call it 'three-pounder'. It and 'Sanna' always had duels resulting in very little success for either side, just like a fight between two bulls of the same age. Three pounds against ninety-four — can anything be funnier? Now just imagine the former being reinforced by three times seven and you have an idea of the duels that ensued. People who in the morning were frightened out of their wits, had an opportunity of turning out and watching the artillery duel. The State Artillery with proper soldiers directly under their nose had no time to think of shelling a town full of unarmed people, and we walked about as freely as if we were in Cape Town, for they warmed up the Boers until about dusk. While she was in the west this morning, the 12-pounder managed to kill a volunteer in the White fort.[7] Whilst they were beckoning the stretchers with a Red-Cross flag the gun sent three shells into the Women's Laager. A fragment of the first killed a child of Mrs Erasmus, Prosecutrix in the Regina versus Emily Bezuidenhout theft of £90, and wounded a little boy so fearfully that he is not expected to live. Ma-Mokoloi died today in hospital. This has been an unfortunate day for both man and beast. Two horses were wounded in town, three cows and a goat killed near the Stadt, and Mr Bell's cow received a Mauser bullet in her neck. Poor dame! This is the second Mauser on the neck since the Siege. Another shell burst in the south; we wonder how long this is going to last. Instead of getting brighter, the prospect in front of us is darkening itself. I am inclined to believe that the Boers have fully justified their bragging, for we are citizens of a town of subjects of the richest and the strongest empire on earth and the Burghers of a small state have successfully besieged us for three months — and we are not even able to tell how far off our relief is. It is certain that it cannot be too near. As the last dispatches told us that the

Boers were at Stormberg, Cape Colony and as far down as Estcourt in Natal, this is a capital stroke and fully justified their bragging. It is a shame on the part of the Imperial Government to 'kgotla semane' [8] before they have tested their abilities to face it.[9] Now they let us square the account while they lounge on couches in London City, reading their newspapers and smoking their half-crown (2/6) cigars. It is a difficult thing to maintain a bright face when so many are ruining your cheer. In the month of October, the British had been victorious against the Boers – so victorious that we were under the impression that the Natal chaps will line the border from the 1st of November. Instead of that being the case, the Boers have since beleaguered Ladysmith and gone traversing the British territory to as far down as Estcourt. Their progress had, according to the last dispatches, not yet been checked.

### Thursday, 4th

A very quiet day. I was a broken reed all yesterday, and a man from Maritzani [10] arrived just in time to pull me together.[11] All of the Boers in the district have rebelled [12] with the sole exception of Mr Vos. The latter, a very kind old Dutchman was our field cornet at Maritzani. He had been arrested three times and taken to the laager, and on each occasion swore that he will never take arms against the English, even if they wish to shoot him. They have allowed him to go on each occasion. When my informant left Maritzani, however, he had received his final notice: that if he adheres to his views, all of his stock would be taken and he and his children sent away to Mafeking. He told me a lot more – that the Troops had fought at the Vaal River. They have previously been travelling to and fro between Kimberley and the Vaal. Since the fight the Boers are not able to tell where they are. Letters have been received at Maritzani from the laager – that there is no use in fighting the English. They always wish to clear away, but are still there – only in obedience to orders; and various other interesting items.

What makes me to believe everything he says is that he heard of the Game Tree fiasco on Saturday last week. They told him that there was a fight in Mafeking in which the Boers lost 27 men and, it is believed, the English lost many more.

### Friday, 5th

It was raining softly all night, and the result is a fair and lovely morning.

The Presiding Officer at the trial of the girl Bezuidenhout, His Honour Major H. J. Goold-Adams, being indisposed, she was remanded sine die.

Poor Ngidi came in for a very rough time. He was before the Court yesterday on a charge of being asleep while on sentry duty the previous night, and was sentenced to be dismissed. He appeared again this morning on a charge of failing to hand over a bag of Kaffircorn. The sentence of the court: seven days H.L.[13] and the confiscation of the Kaffircorn. Hard luck on poor little Alfred. The following is the cause of his trouble: during the month of November the authorities, deeming it expedient in view of the approaching hard times, forbade the sale of grain of any sort by the storekeeper. All grain belonging to storekeepers was commandeered, and the government had it retailed cheaply – on economic lines – to the public.

For this purpose they have established a grain store in the Stadt, one at the location, and Lippman's in town. Early in December orders were issued to private owners as well that they were to state the amount of grain in their possession, as this drain got a grip of us; and it became imperative that all grain should be collected from private people, and everybody be allowed to buy so little as not to have the slightest chance of wasting anything. It is only by dint of a favour that I was allowed to buy a steen brood [14] per diem. Therefore it is criminal to have in your possession any quantity of grain beyond what the regulations permit you to purchase from one of these stores run on economical lines.[15]

Rice, barley, oatmeal, and sugar [16] have also been included and their sale is restricted unless one has an order which regulates the quantity he can purchase in a certain shop to last him a certain period. A common person would be enriched by this arrangement, as cash cannot procure whatever one requires – he being allowed to purchase so much worth and the balance all remaining in his till. But our [17] case is different: the regulation diet is cheap enough as the purchase price is also regulated, but it is too small to keep a decent man alive. One can only increase his diet by various unrestricted luxuries, the prices of which rule higher than the clouds.

From an official's viewpoint, this restriction is a wise policy, as it prevents the decrease of our supplies from passing faster than the days of the Siege. To the merchant it is a boon, in as much as it enables him to demand whatever he desires for his unrestricted dainties. It is a curse however, in that the money is circulated at the expense of the private individual's pocket.[18]

From a Serolong [19] point of view this whole jumble is more annoying than comforting. For this they may be excused, as the arrangement is in the hands of young officers who know as little about Natives and their mode of living as they know about the man on the moon and *his* mode of living.

It came to their notice that some Barolongali [20] were selling kaffir beer the other day. They look upon it as wasting, or if the scale of this luxury was to continue, they were going to make a case against the party and would have, had the Civil Commissioner not been what he is – a White Native.

They do not know that kaffir beer to a common Morolong is 'meat vegetables and tea' rolled into one, and they can subsist entirely on it for a long time. If ever you wish to see the sense of the word economy, observe the kaffir beer by the amount of water poured into the corn to what is yielded. If prohibited, I wonder what is to become of the bachelor, who is a fighting man and soldier and can therefore not brew it for himself, as it is not sold in any of the three.[21]

The collection of grain is now going on in the Stadt unlike at the location. There it is carried away [22] by the chiefs. The officers are under the impression that when the chiefs reach a hut they take away the last crumb they find in possession of the owner, who would henceforth survive on what they purchase economically from the store. The store has been shut for the last five days, because when the regulation was struck down to 6$d$ a time, Barolongali told the storeman he could go to H. This was last Sunday. The store has since been shut. I believe the storeman has gone to Hopetown in obedience to the Black Petticoat Ordinance.[23] I presume the truth is that the officers are either under the impression the Barolongs are able to purchase from a closer store, or that they can live a week without – for otherwise I cannot comprehend. This causes me to believe that they liken Barolongs to the man in the moon, who is at his place every time there is a full moon. The full moon is always at night, when the store is closed, and the man in the moon could not possibly come down for any grain; and it is their belief that Barolong can do the same: for while this 'every-morsel-economical-collection' is in progress, the store shows no sign of reopening – God help these poor beleaguered people.

Ebie has a very bad chest. He has had it for the last few days and he shows no sign of improving. His people 'ncoma'[24] his coughing as that which was never heard in the hut before. Most of the children are down with fever. Further, Molema's cattle and many others have the Rinderpest. Mafeking [25] has 'setlhabi'[26] – she can hardly breathe. Sickness has formerly not troubled us very much during the Siege; sickness was so rare that I have never heard anyone complain of toothache.

With Selabi all the afternoon. He told me of the welfare of my family. If he is not the boldest 'cheat'[27] in Bechuanaland, I owe him an apology.

Since [28] the middle of the last month we have been tasting to see if the Civil Commissioner's grapes are ripe; so far we have only been able to discover that they are sweet, but we cannot yet tell if they are ripe or green. There is, however, no likelihood of this being found out until there are no more grapes to taste!

This morning I went round for another taste. I tried to pick only as much as necessary for tasting, when the whole bunch came down on my hand – rather a heavy weight. It weighed about three pounds, but I was not the fool to replace it, although it was far too much more than I required. In the afternoon I saw the 'baas'[29] filling his little basket and I went round for another 'discovery' viz. what they taste like. Just when I came in, I heard [30] 'Do you know who steals my grapes, Patrick?' I carried on bravely: 'No, Sir, I don't.' 'Do you know Plaatje?' 'I am Plaatje. 'Do you know who always steals my grapes?' 'No.' 'To steal is no answer . . . By Jove! It is you who always steals my grapes. Can't you fellows do without stealing?'[31]

I thought that the next question might be too unpleasant and I tried to modify the flowing tide before it grew worse, so I began:

'I have only been eating ("eating" mind you and not "stealing") those in front of the stable, Sir.'

'I don't see why you should steal them even if they were at the back of the stable, for your father [32] didn't steal my grapes.'

I successfully stemmed the tide when I interpolated:

'Well, my father didn't work for the Magistrate.'

He turned around and went on with his business. He was still smiling when he eventually gave me the sweetest bunch in the garden!

*Saturday, 6th*

About a dozen or more of the location people have been summonsed to appear before the Court of Summary Jurisdiction on Monday morning next. (They include the Lumata and M'Fazi families, and other prominent locationists.) They must answer to a charge of having wrongfully, unlawfully and maliciously neglected to hand over their grain when requested by the authorities to do so. Things are getting serious. Today was very quiet. We had only two shots from 'Sanna' during the day but the smaller fry was brisk – the smaller the brisker – late in the afternoon. At six o'clock there was a perfect fusillade, and Mauser bullets flew, zip-zip-zip, about the town in the same manner as they did in November last. Everyone wondered what was up.

There have been certain smashes [33] in town during this week, and everybody is tired of the Siege. I am afraid some people will be too far gone to be able to welcome our relief when it turns up. It rains nearly every day, but softly enough to keep things in good order.

*Sunday, 7th*

The usual thing; joy, pleasure, merryment, sports, etc. etc. I met

Miss Ngono this morning. I had not seen her for a month, and she was so broken-hearted that when I looked at her face I thought it was starvation telling on her constitution – but the following was the cause: her lover was a member of MacKenzie's Black Watch. Whilst out sniping he received [a wound] in the head. He appeared to be recovering, but certainly grew worse at the beginning of this week and ultimately died the other night. The poor girl is simply thrown on her own resources. Rev. F. G. Briscoe left for Cape Town several months ago without paying her that quarter's salary. Mr Peard, of the town Wesleyans, appears to have exchanged the church for a Lee-Metford and the poor girl must see how she can manage it.

### Monday, 8th

A very quiet day – fair and cloudy. It rained softly all the afternoon. Cannoning was mild and Mausering nil. A little boy named Phalaetsile escaped from the Boers yesterday. A poor chappie of only about 7 years old, he found himself accidentally in the hands of the Boers three Sundays ago. Some volunteers are always moved from one end of the camp to the other, and he was one of the youngsters that always carried their blankets [34] for a sixpence and part of their rations. They were out looking for a similar job about our farthermost redoubts, when he and a companion played into the hands of the Boers. He has since been employed as a herd in the Big Gun fort. I am afraid we have seldom had so much news, [even] from a fellow five times his age. He really has sympathy for Britain in his little heart. He made an earthen plan of the Big Gun fort – with sand and pieces of wood showing the position of the tents, wagons, and horses in it, and also the action of the Big Gun – so cleverly that the Colonel came to study it. He states there were two artillery duels lately. After the first, two Boers were killed and one had his left arm broken; after the second he found 5 dead Boers, but he cannot state if there were any wounded. He says the chief gunner was shot during last week and knocks about with the crutch. I asked him why he [35] doesn't lie down when he is wounded. He said 'Kaitse ke ene ba shupetsang fa toropo e sekgotlho e teng.'[36]

He tells a whole lot of interesting items. He states that during last week someone rode from the head laager to say that the English wrote to say that they shouldn't fire at the Hospital. On hearing this the gunners fired 2 shots at the Hospital on purpose. Official Publication adds that these are the two shots that fell very close to the Hospital on the 2nd Inst. There is so much about this interesting little boy that I will never forget. The Colonel came round to the Residency for the sole purpose of studying his earthen plan of the Big Gun fort.

### Tuesday, 9th

Shelling was very mild. I cannot say if it was in consequence of the long 'medupe'[37] that rained nearly the whole day. 'Sanna' didn't fire a single shot today. Some fellows came with three oxen they lifted from the Boers. They had another row with MacKenzie's Black Watch. MacKenzie's Black Watch are nonsensical and their action is tantamount to doing the enemy more good than harm; it cannot be said otherwise, for if people are treated harshly on their arrival no-one will care to go for more cattle and the Boers, of course, would benefit in that case.[38]

It was only when a party of young Barolong, prompted by the injustice done to them, challenged them with their rifles, that the Black Watch yielded to their taking the cattle away – but not before they had wounded two of them. (Cattle, not Barolongs.)

### Wednesday, 10th

Things were somewhat quiet today, but Boer fire was somewhat effective. An innocent man was tapping some water out of a tank when a Mauser bullet entered his body by the neck, coursed through his inside, and exited through his left loin. He was stooping down at the time, and stood straight and walked about a little before he was taken to the Hospital on a stretcher; and died about 5 hours later. I have also heard of a white woman being killed during the day.

### Thursday, 11th and Friday, 12th

These have been very funny days. Boers hammering away at us in a most extraordinary manner. Goodness knows what provoked them. Three more fellows went out to look for stock.

### Saturday, 13th

We woke to find that my wife has a splendid birthday. A very quiet morning, Mausering conspicuous in its silence. A quiet and beautiful day – almost no hammering by the Big Gun; only the distant puff-puff-puff-puff of the Nordenfeld tells that there is no rest for the friend and that there is trouble for the foe. Three fellows, who went out to loot stocks, had come back this morning with 20 heads of cattle – big fat elephants.

The Colonel has ruled a new Proclamation that every man in Mafeking with looted cattle should pay the Government the fourth part of whatever he brought in. He would have nothing to do with the oxen, however, and is quite right, for surely if that was the case fewer men would care about going for cattle – and this is calculated to do the enemy more good than harm. Besides, by taking the cattle away from the enemy, a man is assisting the authorities – and why should the authorities come round and fine a man for having helped them? It was like ten weddings in the Stadt today. Each of the principal 'kgotlas'[39] being supplied with an ox, we had some swagger dinner – roast beef and the rarest vegetables, and various other dainties.

We had arranged for the purchase of a sheep and kaffir-beer to be used at Mathlaseloa's redoubt (this is everything to them) in honour of the occasion of the birthday of Lethlaseloakazi. But we only purchased the latter cheap stuff,[40] meat being too plentiful to warrant a farther expenditure on a sheep. So I sat down and looked on, while the bulk stirred themselves. Such rejoicing never took place in the Stadt since there was such a thing as rinderpest.[41] My only trouble was now and then to tell a friend that this is my wife's birthday – and that joy is doubled.

P.S. The following shows that there is a very great difference between white and black even in a besieged town: 'Fresh meat rations to be reduced to $\frac{3}{4}$ lbs. from Monday inclusive.' It is a notice by Capt. Ryan, D.A.A.G., to the townites.[42]

*Sunday, 14th*

The big gun is away from its fort. Many people say it has left us for good, but I am inclined to the belief that they have moved further away as their present position is very dangerous [being] under a continuous shellfire from our little Nordenfeld. If I was in their place I would have moved it back soon after the first fellow fell, as there is no necessity for losing any life when I can bomb-shell my enemies from a distance far out of their range – as is the case with the big gun. Bets are in circulation that the Boers have taken it away to Pretoria. They, however, didn't remain undecided for a long time, for in the afternoon it was discovered that they had shifted it across the river to a spot about $3\frac{1}{2}$ miles east – alongside the road to Madikwe. I wonder how they will shoot at us in the morning as they cannot get at a quarter of our town from where it is. I hope they will not merely send shells into the place without aiming at anything.

The plentiousness of our pantry since yesterday causes us to keep up a birthday with the Mahlelebes today. That Mr Bell is given half of one ox is sufficient sign that this is not yet the last of it.

*Monday, 15th*

'Sanna' has been removed from her fort and is shelling from another position near MacMullen's.[43] She gave her debut on the Madikwe road at noon today. One thing that frightened me very much yesterday was whether it will be sufficiently in sight for them to give us the warning. But the alarm bells still rang as they used to do: a ring, two strokes, to warn us that she is loaded and that she is pointed to the south of the camp; and six strokes, to the north. Then a lively gentle finale or 'pasop'[44] when we all dodge into our holes. So my alarm is alert.

The first shell went for a hut at the edge of the Stadt. It was quite new and strongly built. It blew the wall clean away, scattered the furniture in every direction and made a way for the reeds, thatched roof and poles to come down to the ground as neatly as though the hut was made like that.

Fortunately no-one was inside. Fragments flew all over the neighbourhood, but beyond filling some pots of kaffir-beer with sand next door, it injured no-one.

## Tuesday, 16th

'Sanna' is exceptionally [active] nowadays. Her new position is extremely dangerous to both the Residency, where I stop most of the day, and the Courthouse, where the Summary Jurisdiction Court sits; all shells have their courses almost invariably over the two roofs. When a shell flies about 20 ft. above the roof you imagine that it will graze your hair. It must, therefore, be worse than nasty when one of her shells flies only 20 inches above the roof, and smashes next door as one did during the day. In the afternoon it went for the Convalescent Hospital in the Railway Institute. Fortunately the sick people were in shelters, so besides wounding a waiter who happened to be about, it played havoc with the furniture. This secondary hospital has since been removed to the Victoria Hospital under cover of the Red Cross. Many of the places knocked about today are not within sight of the big gun. They merely plug shells into the place without knowing what they are going for. A spy has been arrested – on Friday. He admitted that he came from the Boers for purposes of spying, and he is now at the gaol awaiting his fate.

## Wednesday, 17th

Summary Jurisdiction Courts are menaced. Shells select the roof of the Courthouse for their course exactly at the Court hours, and keep smashing the neighbourhood.

## Thursday, 18th

Boers are using some marvellous shells just now. Experts say that they are very new and must be made in Johannesburg. I wonder if the gunners who fire them appreciate the idea that they are better and deadlier than the brand 'Made in Germany'. They seldom burst where they first land, but merely plough the ground for a little distance, then pump right up in the air again and start a fresh journey for one or two more miles before they reach their fag end. This afternoon they sent a shell in the direction of the Market Square. It went through the office of the *Mafeking Mail*,[45] frightened the compositors out of their wits, went into D. Webster's next door, and burst just on top of Vere Stent's bomb-proof. A fragment pierced the wall of Dixon's bar, touched up the head of the proprietor a bit, and scattered the bottles all over the floor. This morning another paid an intrusive visit to the other end of the Market Square and thundered into Lippman's store, completely ragging his office and the goods therein. Little Mr Lippman was choked with dust when he came out, and could hardly apprehend the sympathetic expression directed to him by the bystanders. He was only coughing like 'kgomo ea ntaramane'[46] for about fifteen minutes. One piece hurt the arm of a young lady, fortunately not seriously, and the crowd of purchasers escaped unhurt. In the evening they fired two heavy volleys with 3 minute intervals between them; the second one was heavier than 'Sanna's' report.

### Friday, 19th

They were firing at our labourers last night. A shell burst in the town hall today. The Bechuanaland Rifles stay there, and a few of them were buried in sand and bits of brick. Others came out with slight shock, but fortunately none were hurt. One shell flew over Meko's house, found a small hut in a hollow, touched the grass works of this, then bumped right up in the air [and] passed over the whole of the Stadt. [It] passed over the Limestone Fort [47] and burst a little way to the west of it.

In the evening, at 9.15 there was a perfect fusillade during which 'Sanna' fired her 'bad-night'. Volleys were fired by the enemy, and kept up incessantly for some time. I believe it was going to last till midnight, had not our 7-pounder in the river bed sent a couple of 'bumps' at their rifle flashes — which partly quenched their metal. Half a dozen puffs-puffs from our Nordenfeld produced dead silence. I believe it has 'jumped-up' many of them, as the shots were aimed at their rifle flashes, and no 'shut-up' was ever so abrupt.

### Saturday, 20th

Shelling-shelling-shelling — the monotony of the day. The Court of Summary Jurisdiction is held on the west of the Courthouse outside, in consequence. A big shell struck the abdomen of the town's Special Constable and fractured his private parts in a most pitiful manner. He is however expected to pull through. Sterk [48] Morolong.

### Sunday, 21st

Today is the celebration of the 100th day of the Siege. People are having all sorts of pleasure in honour of the occasion, and one can almost fancy it is their desire to celebrate a 200th day.

Teacher Samson is very ill at the location. He has the rheumatic fever – the result of a bad cold his foot contracted while guarding on a rainy night.

This afternoon the Civil Commissioner held a meeting of the Barolongs in the Stadt. Reuter and London *Times* war correspondents were also there. Things went on very smoothly until Wessels commenced to speak. He threw a different complexion on the otherwise excellent harmony which characterised the commencement of the proceedings. He misunderstood, misconstrued and misinterpreted everything said and an undesirable scene ensued.

I think he took serious exception to the suggestion by the Civil Commissioner that whoever desires to leave the place for the time being should be permitted to do so, as our supply of food is too limited. They both kept on talking, and scarcely gave each other a chance, each expecting me to translate his hot beans first. Whoever can interpret for Wessels correctly ought to consider himself a professor. Fancy having to either make an English speech, or to turn every word of the following half-sensible, broken Setswana parts of sentences and phrases, offered after peculiar intervals, into English:

'E' – 'ke a utlwa' – 'ke utlwa sentle' – 'jaka a bua' – 'ke re, morena' – 'a re . . .' [49]

Every one of these sentences causes him to assume a more serious attitude. He will wave to and fro and occasionally change position and chair, or stand up to demonstrate his injured feelings. It is an excellent thing that the C.C. is so patient or else things could happen that would cause great joy in the Boer laager when they became known there.

### Monday, 22nd

The same hammering by the big gun. [It is the] lot of a beleaguered community and we are awfully tired of it.

### Tuesday, 23rd [50]

Shelling same as yesterday; all the shops have been closed as far as concerns the sale of everything edible, and the food is going to be rationed [51] out to the whites the same as the blacks in the grain stores.[52] The foreign women, perhaps, carry their parts with a grumble, but the leaders are announcing an offer for them to buy and [they] will be told that they can purchase tomorrow.[53] They say they will send back their tickets and ask for one which is available to buy any day.

This morning two were before the Court of Summary Jurisdiction. They were attempting to purchase with tickets belonging to other people. They pleaded ignorance and were dismissed with a caution.

## Wednesday, 24th

There is a Proclamation by the Colonel R. S. S. Baden-Powell that no food stores of any kind would in the future be sold to the public;[54] and white people are now going to buy food in rations and be compelled to buy small quantities, the same as blacks. I have often heard the black folk say money is useless as you cannot eat it when you feel hungry, and now I have lived it and experienced it. The thing appears to be going from bad to worse. The big gun is still hammering away at us. It was particularly cruel today. One of its shells hit on the Market Square this morning. It bumped right up in the air and singled out old Moshuchwe's hut (one-and-a-half-miles away); after its decline it entered the hut from the back, decapitating two women and wounding three brothers severely and one not dangerously. The old boy was not there.

## Thursday, 25th

Today was somewhat quiet. The Boers appeared to be short of Mauser ammunition. Sniping was not nearly as brisk as it was a month or two ago. At 2 p.m. Mafikeng [55] sent me some lovely stew and a few eggs for my supper in the evening. It arrived just while we were preparing our dinner and the former added to it just made up what one might call a splendid meal; and it was the same thing with the supper in the evening. Raseleye [56] kept repeatedly saying that he wondered why we are so lucky with food to have it falling into my direction; as it was the second anniversary of my wedding we enjoyed it all the more.

## Friday, 26th

Malno arrived this morning but has greatly disappointed me as he has recently been to Kimberley. Finding the river impassable, he handed his dispatches to Mr Honey of Skaapdam,[57] but he brought me a letter from the Imperial Government with the sad news of Ntsala Sakaria's demise.[58] This is particularly [unfortunate] coming as it does during Ebie's serious indisposition, and I am left to mourn his loss quietly by myself. The letter does not state when he died.

## Sunday, 28th

The usual thing. In the middle of the morning the tranquillity of the neighbourhood was severely marred by the tolling of the warning bell. There was such a rush from town as has never . . .[59]

EDITORIAL NOTE

For the townspeople of Mafeking events took a serious turn for the worse during the month of January. For the first time the diarist conveys a mood of frustration; his attention is drawn increasingly to the civilian situation, its pathos and its bitterness. The many diaries kept during the period show neither the determined spirit of October and November, nor the (sometimes forced) cheerfulness of December. They speak rather of boredom and of growing physical hardship.

Whether or not Plaatje is right about the inexperience of the officers organising the production and distribution of food, it is interesting to speculate on how the encouraging situation of October gave way suddenly to the need for frantic organisation of supplies in January. The food situation was symptomatic: many essential commodities were now being requisitioned. But the shortage was not restricted only to necessities. Equally threatening, albeit from a different point of view, was the shortage of ammunition. Remarkable work was undertaken by the ordnance workshop in this respect. Anything that had potential use as an explosive was suitably modified, and two artillery pieces were built. One was made with the gatepost from Rowland's Farm as its primary component; this curious object turned out to be an eighteenth-century, sixteen-pound naval gun, and after a clean-up was mounted and christened 'Lord Nelson' in honour of its seafaring past. The other, the 'Wolf', was constructed under the inspiration and direction of the artillery commander, Major Panzera. Like the gatepost gun, it turned out to have a longer range than expected. Together they were used to expand the perimeter of the besieged area so as to gain greater access to the desperately needed pasturage across the line of investment.

Slowly but inexorably the internal pressures on the garrison mounted. As they did so, the Boer commander saw to it that bombardment from outside was intensified. From 1 January shelling had been greatly increased. It was well timed to induce a waning of morale. Yet things were still a long way from their lowest ebb. Sports and entertainments continued to provide the community with an opportunity to present a brave face. Ever faithful to the cause of morale-building, the tone of the *Mafeking Mail* remained cheerful. On the 6th it announced the Relief of Ladysmith. That the report was false did not lessen its effect on the populace – at least, not until its unreliability was proved. But, besides its more encouraging information and announcements of pleasant events to come, reminders of the real situation stood out in grim relief. On the 9th the hoteliers published a notice to the effect that whisky prices were to rise to 1s 6d per glass (with other liquor increasing proportionately). Perhaps with a measure of irony, a 'Grand Agricultural and Produce Show' was announced for Sunday the 21st. The *Thermometer of Hope*, which marked the progress of relief troops on their way towards Mafeking, was rising. It was soon to lift the people to a pinnacle of hope – and then to drop them again into despair.

## CHAPTER NOTES

1 Plaatje is questioning the applicability of the diminutive suffix *je* in the gun's nickname. Why should such a powerful weapon be referred to diminutively when 'Griet' (without the diminutive) would reflect her potency more aptly?

2 Like David, Ebie was a co-resident in the homestead and a friend of the diarist. It is possible to hazard a guess (based on a later entry) that Ebie was a kinsman (perhaps a nephew or a son) of one of the diarist's close friends in Kimberley.

3 Ellitson was the local butcher. Photographs taken during the siege show a tree from which cattle, and later horses, were hung up after slaughter. Judging from the background of these photographs, this tree was sited somewhere on the fringe of the Stadt. It is safe to adduce, therefore, that this was the slaughter pole which Ellitson (probably the unidentified White in the photograph) erected, and to which Plaatje refers here.

4 Dutch: literally 'red-neck'. This was a nickname given to the British by the Boers. It derives from the fact that when light-skinned Englishmen first came into contact with the hot South African sun their skins tended to redden from sunburn. The unprotected neck is particularly sensitive to this, and invariably the men concerned found themselves sporting red napes.

5 Dutch: 'damned' or 'blasted'.

6 Sotho-Tswana: 'become fat'. The implication is that horse meat was mixed into the grain to fatten it, thus providing a more substantial meal.

7 There was no fort named White. Perhaps this refers to the Women's Laager, as the passage immediately following suggests. It is possible that he intended 'Whiteley's fort' — for the Mayor spent much of his time organising and supervising the Women's Laager. That this error of partial omission is likely, we may adduce from the fact that this passage is again in the second handwriting. As before, it is far more careless and primitive than the rest of the text.

8 Tswana: 'to poke at the wasps'. (This is similar to the English phrase 'disturb a hornet's nest'.)

9 The question of Britain's preparedness for war is an interesting and perhaps controversial one. There are many pre-war reports of statesmen, both in England and in Cape Town, denying its possibility and arguing that overt preparation might mean precipitation. We know that Baden-Powell's efforts to equip and train a force had to be done with the utmost discretion. This is why the argument that the Commanding Officer in Mafeking organised the siege to commit Boer troops and thus buy time for Britain cannot be dismissed, but it implied committing 1,200 whites and nearly 10,000 Barolong to the trials of war. Hence it is easy to understand Plaatje's lamentations and recriminations.

10 Maritzani (more commonly spelt Mareetsane) is a village of the Barolong boo Ratshidi and falls under the jurisdiction of their chief. It is situated about twenty-five miles south-south-west of Mafeking.

11 Plaatje seems to have had an insatiable appetite for eliciting news. He was, during the siege, often sick in body and frustrated in mind. But if anything made him feel better it was — as on this occasion — the arrival of information from outside. The juxtaposition here of his statement about his own feelings and the news itself is slightly confusing as he makes no introductory remarks to precede the latter.

12 As Mareetsane fell within the borders of the Cape Colony, allegiance to the Boers was regarded as an act of rebellion against Britain.

13 Hard Labour.

14 Dutch: literally, 'a brick (loaf) of bread'.

15 It is interesting to read one of the reminders printed by the *Mafeking Mail* on the subject. Dated 2 January, it states the following:

Merchants, Traders, Shopkeepers, etc. are prohibited from selling Mealies, Mealie Meal, Kaffir Corn or Grain of any sort. There are three Grain Stores existing at which purchase of Grain can be made, viz.:

No. 1. Native Stadt.

No. 2. Native Location.

No. 3. Lippman's Yard, Town Store (For Townspeople).

It has come to notice that several people who have small quantities of Mealie Meal and Grain in their possession are in the habit of handing over to their servants certain bulk quantities in order that the servants may feed themselves. This causes unnecessary waste. Servants should be put on rations by their masters daily. The following quantities should amply suffice under present circumstances:

1 lb. to 1½ lbs. of Mealie Meal or Grain, proportionate deduction being made when Native women or children have to be fed, such as ½ to ¾ lb. per diem.

C. M. RYAN, Capt.
D.A.A.G.

Mafeking 30th Dec., 1899

16 Another commodity is mentioned, but as it is indecipherable in the text it has been omitted.

17 'Our' here appears to refer to the Barolong and location-dwellers. 'Common person' immediately before probably refers strictly to the whites.

18 The last two sentences (again, it seems, dictated by the diarist to some other scribe) are incoherently phrased. They have been changed around so as to render them comprehensible.

19 Serolong is the language of the Barolong. (It is also used indigenously to mean the culture of the Barolong.) In English conversation 'Serolong' and 'Barolong' are often confused, for their contextual referents are not perfectly translatable.

20 Sotho-Tswana: 'Barolong women'. -*ali* (pronounced -*adi*) is the Sotho-Tswana feminine suffix.

21 I.e., the three grain-stores. Brewing beer is, traditionally, women's work.

22 I.e., collected.

23 It appears that this is Plaatje's own label for the protest by the Barolong women.

24 Xhosa-Zulu: 'recommend', 'praise', 'commend', 'extol'. (The *c* here is a dental click.) The implication is that this was specially remarked upon.

25 'Mafeking' was also the name of a close (female) friend of Plaatje's. Her daughter, Emang, who was a teenager during the siege and is still alive (October 1969), is mentioned again in Chapter 4.

26 Tswana: 'a sudden piercing pain in the chest; *angina pectoris*'. (J. Tom Brown, *Secwana-English Dictionary*, 1931.)

27 This is merely Plaatje's way of saying, with a modicum of tact, that Selabi's story was fabricated. As there is no mention that Selabi was a dispatch runner, it is possible that he was a diviner.

28 From here this entry is written in pencilled shorthand. The script is very faint, but part of the text is written in long hand on the previous page, so that an almost complete translation was possible. (The two entries have been amalgamated to produce the fullest possible version.) Expert opinion has suggested that, judging from the script itself, Plaatje had just learnt the art — but that he was a talented student. There are two possible reasons for this particular entry being written in shorthand: either, as a legally minded citizen, he did not want the reader to know that he was accused of thieving (for that part of

the text is not reproduced in long hand), or he simply wanted to practise the art.

29 The *baas* (Dutch: 'boss', 'master') here could not have been Bell, unless the man had a very perverse sense of humour. It is difficult to guess the identity of the person concerned.

30 There are a few words after this, but they proved too faint to decipher.

31 This shorthand passage ends here. In a few instances the quotation marks are omitted in the text. They have been inserted.

32 He probably meant 'your father's generation' (Plaatje's own father died before the siege and there is no evidence that he ever visited Mafeking).

33 He means 'accidents' or 'setbacks'. The week had, it is true, been unfortunate for the beleaguered. For example: on 1 January a carpenter, Slater, was killed; on the 2nd, a niece of the chief and several others were killed in the Stadt; on the 3rd, two children were killed in the Women's Laager; on the 4th, typhoid broke out in the Women's Laager.

34 The fact that the defending troops were constantly being redeployed gave Barolong youths an opportunity to earn small sums as porters.

35 I.e., the chief gunner.

36 Tswana: 'I knew that he directed them to the town backyard which was there.' The Tswana spelling is interspersed with Sotho orthographic usage. *Sekgotlho* is usually used to describe the rear section of a homestead; hence we translate it as 'backyard'. In fact, the sentence is curiously written; rather than *toropo e sekgotlho*, it should have been *segotlho ea toropo*. Perhaps this reflects the fact that it is a child speaking. Plaatje's young informant was trying to explain that the gunner was the only one who could effectively aim the gun on the town.

37 Sotho-Tswana: 'gentle rain, long continued' (Brown, *Secwana-English Dictionary*, 1931).

38 From this and a previous entry we learn that members of the (ethnically mixed) Black Watch had a habit of apprehending returning cattle-raiders in an attempt to dispossess them of their loot. The authorities were worried about this as a threat to law and order; but Plaatje was concerned for a more fundamental economic reason – the discouraging of suppliers.

39 Sotho-Tswana; *kgotla* has a wide range of meaning. The usual primary translation given is 'council-place' (Brown, *Secwana-English Dictionary*; T. J. Kriel, *New English-Sesotho Dictionary*, 1958). However, in some places *kgotla* is also used to describe political units of various orders, such as wards and sections. (See Schapera, *The Tswana*, 1953). *Kgotlo* also refers to the meeting-enclosure that is usually found in each ward. *Lekgotla* is a 'council', but modern Tshidi tend to drop the prefix *le-*. There is a degree of local variation in the range of meaning that the word covers. Here *kgotlas* (the English plural suffix *-s* replacing the Sotho-Tswana class-five (plural) prefix *ma-*) refers to 'wards'. (For a discussion of these political units, see Schapera, *Handbook of Tswana Law and Custom*, 1938.)

40 I.e., the beer.

41 He refers here to the rinderpest epidemic of 1896 which reduced Barolong herds drastically. Even today it is a historical event which is often recalled – and used to date the people and occurrences of the era.

42 *Mafeking Mail*, 13 January; by this time the situation in the *stadt* was beginning to look very serious and rationing was much tighter than in town. Many of the poverty-stricken survived on the horse-meat soup made by five kitchens: three in the Stadt, one in the location and one in the town. A foul-smelling horse-meat factory was set up south-west of the town. This began to produce everything from brawn and sausages to stuffing for pillows. The popularity of this

food rose in correspondence with the decrease in the availability of alternatives.

43 MacMullen's Farm was about two-and-a-half miles east of town.

44 Dutch: 'watch out' or 'take care'.

45 The *Mafeking Mail* did not publish an edition until the 21st as a result.

46 Sotho-Tswana: 'a head of cattle with (literally, "of") lung sickness'.

47 A perimeter defensive fort to the west of the town.

48 Dutch: 'strong'.

49 Sotho-Tswana: 'Yes . . . I understand (hear) . . . I understand well . . . the way he speaks . . . I say, Sir . . . he says . . .'

50 From here until the end of the month the entries are in shorthand. One reason for this passage being written thus may have been the pressure of time.

51 This was repeated in the Proclamation issued by Baden-Powell on the 21st (which Plaatje mentions in the next entry). The extent of the rationing was announced by Captain Ryan on the same day: 'Full ration, European: Men 2/–, women, half ration, 1s., children under 14, 6d.' This statement is not entirely clear, for we are not quite sure whether this meant that the stated amount could be spent on every occasion that an individual went (by arrangement) to a store. At this time Barolong men (full ration) were permitted to spend 6d.

52 The shops which were permitted to retail foodstuffs under supervision of the authorities.

53 That this is not clear is a result of the fact that the rationing arrangements were still confused. People were, at the time, in the process of registering and receiving ration tickets, and supply-scales had been announced, but the mechanics of distribution were yet to be clarified.

54 The first two paragraphs of the Proclamation read as follows: 'I hereby proclaim and direct that on and after the 21st instant all shops will close for the sale of foodstuffs in any form. Stock lists to be sent to Capt. Ryan, D.A.A.G., of all supplies then on hand and these will be held as strictly in bond for the Imperial Authorities.' (*Mafeking Mail*, 21 January.)

55 Mafikeng (the daughter of Molema, founder of Mafikeng) was married to Lekoko (see entry for 29 December). It was with her brother's family that Plaatje lived during the siege.

56 Probably a friend and neighbour of the diarist, this man is mentioned occasionally during the latter parts of the text.

57 It has proved impossible to obtain any information about this person.

58 No Barolong survivors could remember his name. He may have been an affine or close associate of Plaatje's, but this has proven impossible to ascertain.

59 The entry is unfinished. The alarm that he mentions must have been false, for had the Sunday truce been violated it would have been recorded by one or another of the sources.

# 4  February 1900

*Tuesday, 6th*

Got up this morning and found very lovely weather. 'Sanna' started at 9.00 and sent 3 shells into the town. I got there at 9.00 and met Sgt. Stuart who told me that the second shell burst in the Civil Commissioner's stable and smashed the stable, Whiskey [1] and all — poor fellow. When I got there I only saw his blood and nothing more of him, and a good thing too. A lot of Basutus [2] congregated on the spot, and hardly gave him time to die — so much in a hurry were they of getting his meat. They undoubtedly deprived the Stadt of the best horse, and put me in fix, as I doubt if poor Whiskey was a mere stroke of luck not likely to present itself again. I went to Phitshani,[3] 48 miles from here, with David one evening. He was sent there to get a horse and I merely accompanied him for pleasure. We had intended to be back at 8 o'clock the next morning, in time for court, as I went without leave. We were confident that David would easily perform the feat, or that I might accomplish it if he gave me the fresh horse we found at Phitshane. Poor Whiskey, however, landed me in Mafeking at 8 minutes past 8.00 and David with his two horses was not able to reach Mafeking before 11.30 — more than 3 hours later. I had been obliged to leave him at Libono, nearly 30 miles away; but this was nothing compared with [the] time we went to settle a land dispute between the Boo Ratlou, when the Inspector of Native Reserve kept changing horses for 5 days — during which his horse was having a rest at Kraaipan.[4] It was, however, not able to carry him further than Maritzani on our return, and he had to give up riding and come home from that station by rail, as he could not keep up with me. He reached here at 4 p.m. per rail and I, on Whiskey, an hour after. It remains to be seen if I will be able to replace him.[5]

Mr Bell was saying — 'poor creature. I was so sorry for him. He had not even murmured or done anything of the kind.'

Whiskey's fate was not our only grief today. The party of ten who went out to loot cattle, returned this morning. Their expedition was a lamentable fiasco: it was most successful, though daring, right up to the last stage of its realisation, but then the whole cart full of apples capsized.

They found that the cattle had been moved so deep into the Transvaal [6] that it would be impossible to reach Mafeking on the same night, if you left late in the evening, so they finally determined to tackle them shortly after sunset, and they did so last night. After the herds finished to milk, they went up to the Kraal [7] and demanded its unconditional surrender. They shouted: 'Coang! Coang! ke tsa Morolong. Janong ga itholi ele tsa Maburu! '[8] So saying, they pulled up some poles at the back of the kraal and started driving some cattle out. About 300 heads were outside, when someone shouted that more than sufficient cattle were out already, and they should come away. 3 of the party followed the cattle and the 7 went for the Boers at the homestead, who had, by this time, been pouring a hail of Mauser bullets on the kraal. Our fellows soon silenced the Boers, but remained a little longer in order that the Boers should not know, too soon, which way the cattle went. I have forgotten to mention that the first shot here was fired at a young Dutchman, who was busy giving orders about the milking, and he fell on the spot. When they left, they saw another man lying dead near the kraal. They surely must have wounded some of them, for the fire of our little band silenced all their Mausers. There were also more than 20 heads of cattle lying about which were wounded by the Boers! So that it is not I only who is sorry today, but also a good many in Boer circles; besides, I will get compensation for poor Whiskey, although I preferred his 'isiqu'[9] to money, but who'll pay a Boer for 20 cattle? Oom Paul's bill is already large enough, and he is not likely to pay compensation to anybody, even if the loser prefers money to 20 head of cattle.

Returning to our subject, we will now devote our attention to the 3 fellows who left with the 300 head of cattle. They drove their cattle, thinking that the 7 men would eventually overtake them. They drove the cattle till about 3.30 a.m., when they were very close to Mafeking – within 2 miles of our furthermost trench – and the Boers then stopped the cattle in front. They opened fire on the Boers and fought a desperate battle with good cheer, thinking that their comrades were somewhere behind, and would hurry up and reinforce them if they heard the shots. But this was not the case, and the Boers got the best of the game, as usual.[10] Our plucky 3 fellows had to come home disappointed.

Returning to the 7 fellows, they walked on the track of the cattle, until one of them complained of sore feet. To leave him behind would have been too inhumane, and whilst they still went along, a piece of wood stuck him in the foot, and they extracted it only with much difficulty. This delayed them, so that they weren't able to get on the track of their loot until it slipped out of the hands of the three men, back into the grasp of the enemy. They are confident that the pain and piece of wood in their comrade's foot were caused by Native 'peljase' [11] by which the owner of the farm (A. Lemmert F.C.[12]) is protected. He and his family wear Native charms, and so do many of the Z.A.R. Commandants and Field Cornets. A Native M.D.[13] once got into trouble with his associates through having taught one of them how to use Dolosse.[14]

In the evening a chappie of the Stadt was struck by a piece of shell on the head and is not expected to live. A little boy was out herding cattle and some Boer shot him on his forehead and the bullet came out at the back of his head. If he was struck by a Martini, then he would have been dead already. But a Mauser bullet being so small, he is still breathing.

We [15] have very great difficulty in feeding the Natives. There are about 7,000 [16] of them in the Stadt only, besides those at the location and the servants employed in the town. The grain supply is fast running short and it has been found necessary to stop giving oats to the horses and grind it for human food. Its first issue was this morning. There was a general murmur abroad which we hope by energetic surveyance soon to overcome, and to satisfy the discontented masses.

### Wednesday, 7th

Up early. One gun is going strong in the west. The Boers have a little Maxim out there and this morning they poured a hailstorm of Mauser and Maxim ammunition at Fort Ayr.[17] If they had not been with us for nearly four months we would have imagined they are effecting an entry, but we have had hundreds of similar fusillades before and this cannot result in anything else but the same as before.

Moatholi kindly lent me his Kolbooi [18] temporarily until I get another charger, but I am already tired of him. He is a good horse and 'takes the Bun' as a trippelaar, but is slow – most piteously slow – and required considerable shoving along, which makes one very impatient and causes him to lose temper occasionally; particularly as he likes to stop every time he meets somebody.

The Boers have not done any damage today although there have been some marvellously narrow escapades.[19] Kolbooi feeds at the leg of the stable outside, and when a shell burst exactly 10 yards past the stable it made me think that they are now going to kill every horse I keep. Capt. Fishe of the Town Guard came in shortly afterwards, frightened beyond measure. He was a few feet from the place where it burst.

### Thursday, 8th

There was a little rain about 4.00 this morning and the weather is very enjoyable this morning.

Runners came in from the north. They bring good news as far as concerns Plumer's Forces up north;[20] but nothing fresh from east and south.

'Au Sanna' went off during the middle of the morning but was quiet all day. I hear they were working at her all day. From today no Natives are allowed in town without a pass.[21] There are three classes of Natives viz. permanent employees in town; permanent employees outside the town; and Stadt folk: the former (class one) are registered in the same manner as in Kimberley (the contract ticket) and walk about with a red ticket. I don't quite understand the procedure in class two. Class three receive a yellow ticket from Lekoko and hand it back every time they return from town. I have started keeping an official diary from today, all of the doings in connection with Native Affairs.[22] This is somewhat bothersome as besides this one I am typing Mr Bell's, Dr Hayes' and Capt Greener's simultaneously. I cannot refuse the new gratis job as I am using the office typewriter and share the pay with no-one; particularly as I heard the chief tell the Mayor that every member of this staff from his chief clerk down to the interpreter and every one of them [are] not only disinclined to do any work during the Siege, but generally lodge a solemn protest and wish each to know the reason why he in particular, and not someone else has to do that work.

The [23] people are now receiving oatmeal for food instead of grain which, it is feared, will run short if sure steps are not taken to save it. The oats were intended for horses, but as the horses could eat grass when things grow serious, it is being thought of as human food. There is a general grumble all round here also. The pang has been felt all round, just at this time when folks had appetites. I have developed a marvellously strong appetite. I long for food every evening at 10.00 p.m. and after taking my supper at 7.00 I nearly die during the night if I do not take a cup of cocoa and a few biscuits before going to bed. Things are getting serious and I consider myself lucky for having thought out the thing at the beginning and stuffed my pants with matches and such things as were likely to be called in when things grow serious. I trust I will not number among those who will eat horses if we are not relieved by the end of March.[24]

Ganankoto [25] was for a little time the Civil Commissioner's great favourite. As he was often called: Hanangkutu; Mr One-Leg; Have-No-Nkutu; Habanab's or Have-no-Legs (from heav'n-O-Legs).

*Friday, 9th*

Very quiet day, although the smaller fry appeared to be particularly sharp — i.e. 'Grulle Annie' [26] and Mausers. We had only 3 shells from 'Au Sanna' today.

114

Runners came in from the south (Kimberley). Just strike out the item about Plumer in yesterday's northern dispatches, and you have the news. They told me about Mr Gabriel and family. They were with him as late as last week and his kids had been ill. Bob Moses was in Kimberley with them last month but he is ill. Elizabeth and Sainty [27] at 'Free State'. It is but a pity they [28] have never attempted to see anyone of my relatives in Kimberley after deciding to come to Mafeking.

Although I am always doing my best to satisfy myself without Whiskey, Kolbooi always gives me cause to regret his fate. For instance this evening I was coming from town: there was a small curve behind the hedge at the railway camp round which I wanted to turn him. He was tripelling very fast and as he is loath to turn quickly he ran plump into the wire fence. I 'tlolela' [29] on one side and stood watching him tangling himself with the wire, until I did not for a moment think he would come out with a sound leg. If he was sensible he would take a lesson from today and stop always looking in the air as though he is smoking a cigar. Disobedience was the cause of this mishap.

Mathakgong [30] went out with four others.

## Saturday, 10th

Things are looking mighty blue. Colonel Baden-Powell states he has received a message from Lord Roberts that we will not be relieved for another three months yet and that he has not got any food for any but Barolongs, the white people and fixed residents of the place. He is therefore going to shut up the Town Grain Store, which was only used for Refugees, who came here from Johannesburg before the war, imagining that the war was going to be a matter of days.

He is going to give them only ten days grace after which he is going to close all stores, and also shut the door against their employment at the Defence Works, where gangs of hundreds of them are employed every day and night. These people include Bangwaketse, Bakwena, Zulus, Zambesians, Shangaans, and others too numerous to mention. The Civil Commissioner has suggested that letters be written to Bathoen [31] and he be asked to communicate with Gnl. Snyman requesting him to let his people come out of Mafeking, as he is on friendly terms with the Boers. By this means of course many people including Barolongs who will only be too pleased to go to Kanya can leave this beleaguered place. A letter will also be sent to Colonel Plumer asking him to be in touch with Bathoen at Kanya and arrange with him to give the people some reward for clearing out of here. It was proposed that Major Goold-Adams should write to Bathoen and so should Wessels: the latter however, refused to have anything to do with the thing.

There appears to be something very deadly about second shells. The second shell this morning went into Mr Dall's house. It found him standing near the kitchen and fractured the lower half of his body; only his upper half was alright. This is very sad. It was only yesterday that I was talking with Mr Dall [32] for the first time since the Siege and he said he was wondering where I had been all the four months.

In the evening some of our people (12) from our advance trench, 2 miles south of the Stadt, went out to annoy the Boers. They passed out unobserved and were only fired on their return. They returned the fire and the Boers fled and were quite silent for the rest of the night.

*Sunday, 11th*

Today was just as usual. A man came from Gopane's and reports Snyman had gone up country to fight Plumer as his Dutch opponents were very 'slecht' [33] and generally good for nothing. This afternoon we sent out 4 runners, two in each direction (north and south).

At 11.00, before we turned in, there was a perfect fusillade. It was a Mauser volley and as they were quickly followed by Martinis we became confident that it was Mathakgong coming in. As they continued, the Mausers remained silent and our belief was firm. Mr Raseleye ran across and found the whole plain alive with armed men making for the scene of operations. And our belief was only too true. He was coming in with 12 head, and on approaching, found that the Boers were themselves on two sides, and had presumably, sworn that it was the 'Verdomde Kaffers' fag end, for directly the cattle was exactly between, they opened fire with heavy volleys from right and left. 4 men returned the fire on the right, and Mathakgong that on the left. What do you think the lot of Boers did? They ran away.

Their volleys wounded two oxen – one fell on the spot and the second fell just inside our advance trench. First class beef for our snipers and Mathakgong brought home ten. These few were all they could find about Maritzani, all of the Boer cattle having been moved deep into the Transvaal. They were probably a span of oxen which strayed from their wagon. May God have mercy on their Native herd!

*Monday, 12th*

This is the hottest day we have had for a long time. Shelling was very mild during last week and all was quiet till after nine this morning. They probably had a Raad [34] about the cattle that came in, as I am sure their number was put down at 50 or 70 and the number of the escort ditto – for surely if they told Snyman that the cattle were driven by only five men they would receive a thrashing and be branded as cowards – to allow only five Kaffirs to pass their lines with cattle! The big gun opened after 9.00 and did its level best to hit numbers of cattle grazing south of the Molopo – and failing to hit them, it went for the town. Presumably with the object of giving us Cayenne Pepper and Mustard to add to the ox meat we were having, but without result. The only casualty for the day was one with far reaching effect. While Mr (now Captn) Girdwood, in charge of the supplies etc., was coming from his home [he] received a bullet in the stomach and is not expected to live longer than a day. Mr E. K. Grayson B.A. has been appointed in his place.

There was a heavy fire all round about the Boers, which gave us the opinion that our runners will not get through, and so it proved, for they all came back this morning. The Brickfields. . . .[35]

## Tuesday, 13th

Captn Girdwood died today. He was a very old Mafekingite, having been a Customs Officer even for the Imperial Government before the Annexation.[36] He was appointed to take charge of the food only a month ago, and he did his best to bring about a desirable satisfaction amongst the Barolong. To attain that object, he sent the storeman away, and introduced a very good-natured fellow who gets along with Barolongs in a most excellent manner. They are most sorry at his death.

The Boers have brought another kind of shell to bear on us. They have incensed[37] the 9-pounder shells and they are very incendiary.[38] Yesterday we saw a flame in the course of one of the shells [in the air] to where it exploded. The flame went out before it reached the ground. These shells struck at Mrs Stenson's, and the explosion caused fire. That must be the reason why they have started shelling the Stadt – apparently to test its effect on the grass thatched huts. They continued the shelling till 10 p.m. and knocked off, presumably disgusted, for no damage was done, and they have become mild again. They are, I think, perfectly convinced that there is nothing in them, for if they were of any use, and if the flames were effective, they certainly ought to have seen the grass huts blaze away in the dark night. However, after one of those shells exploded, Manomphe's son-in-law, Thlaping, walked up, and while picking up a fragment, noticed that there was something like a cut diamond[39] in the debris. He picked up this beauty of a thing. His nerve, however, told him that there was danger in it but, in order to do justice to his pluck, he took his left hand full of sand, and put this thing on it. The sand caught fire and burnt his hand. He chucked away this thing and rubbed his burning left hand with his right. The former ignited the latter, and he was soon tortured with pain. His only relief is to keep his hands in cold water – this does not help much unless fresh water is put in every three minutes, for the water becomes very hot after it.

*Wednesday, 14th*

Ebie's birthday — I have not done anything for it, as I have since night before last got a most excruciating pain in the foot. I never thought rheumatism had such a sharp pain. I have been writing this all through it.

The Colonel sent a hot message to Lekoko saying that he and his people did very wrong in slaughtering the cattle [40] without giving the Commissariat a chance of buying any of them. His answer was no 'cooler'. 'We have been giving you a fourth of all the loot, and you said you did not care for it.' [41]


*Thursday, 15th*

Today was like the day on which the big gun arrived. Consternation was written in bold and expressive type in the face of everybody in the Stadt. The gun had been moved from its position round to the south-west of the Stadt, about 5 miles away, and therefore $6\frac{1}{2}$ miles from town. The Limestone Fort, Women's Laager, and the Stadt are therefore going to be its restless victims.

It tested its range at about 10.30 and fell short of the Limestone Fort. No. 2 burst unpleasantly aside of the fort, and 3 made head for the Stadt; 4 missed Mamolateli; 5 and 6 plumped into the Women's Laager and 7 went for the old Wessels (Senobi's) house. It smashed the passage shelter, killing 2 Bangwaketse women, who happened to be about, and wounding one. All the others fell promiscuously about the Stadt. These shells came in rapid succession, and at noon there was 2 hours' respite. At 2 p.m. they sent over 2 more, which failed to reach town. At 5 p.m. they sent their last, which fell in the Stadt, and fortunately did not burst.

Thus was the debut of 'Au Sanna's' undesirable entertainment. They loaded after five, but although the bells kept us expectant she was quiet for the evening. I am inclined to the belief that the spot they have chosen lastly is uncomfortable for them. 3 miles was a bad range for them from which to try to hit the town, but $6\frac{1}{2}$ miles is still worse. We surely cannot understand why the Boers should go and place the gun so far away — and that on the further side of the Transvaal border. The general idea is that nothing is daunting them and they see that it stands in absolutely no danger whatever of being molested, and completely drives away all expectations of relief for us.[42] But there is something else. There was a flag of truce coming from Snyman's laager. One Cape Policeman went to meet it. It was a message from Snyman and the bearer of it told our policeman that there had been a serious battle in Natal! On our man asking who took the day the bearer said he did not know: this message said the writer has instructed the Burghers that if in future the inhabitants expose themselves on Sundays they should fire on them. One can almost think that he is going to Kimberley with the big gun on Sunday and does not want us to see a considerable portion of his laager trekking.

*Friday, 16th*

The Stadt has [for] once changed from its usual appearance and assumed a sullen aspect. We have not experienced it yet, but if the long look for the greatest day is unequalled, today was undoubtedly a second study of Judgement Day. People were almost disinclined to talk to one another, and there was dead silence in the green shrubbery which almost gave one the impression that on other days they were talkative. I spent my day in Old Watemann's garden without food of any sort: it was only [when] she, grand lady, brought me several sweet cones [that I could] break my fast. I felt very stimulated after being invigorated by them and tired of novel reading and shorthand exercises. I still retained a fresh enough memory to picture to myself the figure of a very young mother and a fat little piccaninny disturbing her peace (assisted by the absence of someone) somewhere about the Eastern Province.[43]

Shelling was going on very lively, and fully justified the people's looks in the morning. The big gun only put in a few, but the show was generally kept up by the incendiary 9-pounders which put in about 30 during the day. It fired from Jackal Tree where it was on the morning that it killed poor Mamokoloi. It, however, went for our defence works like it ought to do. It went almost invariably for the forts of McKenzie's Black and the Barolong Watches – within 2 miles of the Stadt. The former is on the railway line and the latter one mile west of it.

Only the big gun went promiscuously for the Stadt, and one woman at my friend Moathloli's house was only saved [from being decapitated] by a hairsbreadth. The shell smashed the wall of the hut, burst inside it then found means of exit through another wall behind which the woman was sitting. One piece burst right opposite her head, but unlike the others it rebounded and fell inside. When the woman bowed her head a lot of earth fell from it and there was a hole in the wall.

The 'bad-night' shot was fired at 8.45. Emang[44] had brought us tea early in the evening. At 8.00 I went home with her. I found Mafikeng sitting near the north-eastern corner of her house against the rising moon. We had not yet chatted to our heart's content when there was heavy rifle firing to the west. We had hardly passed remarks over it when 'tingalingalingaling' chimed the 'toesins'[45] and we dodged like a couple of meercats. There was a heavy suspense when we were waiting for the blow – I think 20 seconds – when bang went a terrible smash. Then the usual row, terminating in a loud explosion that echoed through all the neighbourhood. Nothing would induce Mafie to remain to the open air and I believe she wanted to be dismissed for directly I suggested she should take to the shelter she leapt and bounded towards it with no less alacrity than Malibali or Emang [46] could have mastered. I went round to see what [it] was like inside. The whole family was arraigned in it. There was old Masiaho, the two girls and two old dames, and goodness knows too what more. This refuge was luminated with a candle that the old dame had sent Mamoathloli for just one hour previously. I strolled back to our quarters and jotted down these notes, while the evening was kept up by the usual rifle chatter which is forever the case in bright moonlight.

### Saturday, 17th [47]

Our troops kept up fire all night. The Maxim was going nobly all the time. By midnight it had become one of the grandest nights, watching our rifle flashes like a lot of fireworks to the south. Our volleys going for the Boers all night were worth listening to. We were pressing away all night: the bright moonlit night being kept alive by the bomb[s] of the 7-pounders [and] Nordenfeld, the cracks of rifles, and the tat-tat-tat of the firing. The Boers had worried the souls out of us during the day;[48] and it is particularly consoling to see that they did it at the expense of their rest the next night. Not a single Dutch weapon was to be heard above the occasional Mauser or rifle.

We had a very quiet day. One often wondered if they exhausted themselves yesterday. 'Au Sanna' sent in a few shells to the Women's Laager.

### Sunday, 18th [49]

The usual thing. Runners came in from up north-east and south. They brought no news. It is difficult to describe one's feeling hearing that even now after four months Kimberley has not yet been relieved. The Imperial Government may be as good as we are told it is, but one thing certain is that [it] does not care a hang over the lives of its distant subjects. It is distressing to hear that Troops are still having a holiday at Modder River,[50] even now after we had been besieged over four months. In Kimberley, which is only a stone's-throw from Cape Town, they were still eating horse-flesh with 10,000 troops at Modder River, and we may safely conclude that we, as far away as Mafeking, will have no more horseflesh to eat by the time they reach here.

The cattle and green mielie stocks have also been called in. No one is allowed to pick any green mielies for his or her village. They are going to be kept till they are ripe and then rationed out to people.

I am wondering if the heavens, like the Imperial Government, have also shut their ears to our prayers. Surely: 'Eare bo bisa go bitsa motho, go bitse molimo.' [51] But was this [so] in our case?

I have a very strong appetite just now when food is very scarce. If I do not take a cup of cocoa at 10 p.m. (after suppering in the evening at 7) you may depend upon it I will never be able to sleep. This is an undesirable bad habit, and I almost feel inclined to consult the medico about it.[52]

## Monday, 19th

As quiet as last Saturday. 'Sanna' only sent in two shells (7 a.m.) which fell short of the town. The day was uneventful.

## Tuesday, 20th

When the pass law was introduced for the time being I expected we would have about 20 convictions every week. We have up to date not had any infringers before the court. In fact when one is found minus the pass the policemen simply tell him to clear out of town.

'Au Sanna' sent in three miserable shots this morning. I believe there is something wrong with her. Only one of them burst and some people mistook the explosion for a Krupp 9-pounder's. One of them went into Moathloli's again but did no damage.

One medico of Mafeking (Dr Smyth) was, at the commencement of the row, appointed to doctor over the inmates of the Women's Laager. He had the funks and declined the appointment fearing to leave his bomb-proof any day except Sundays. He has since been living at his house, which was also struck by a 94-pounder last week. I wonder where he intends going.

## Wednesday, 21st [53]

A calm and unusually lovely day! Eventually I got up early and went to town, returning at 12, and spent the day in the gardens. Joshua caught a thief in these gardens. He was a heathen, and in a farmer's employ. They nearly beat him to death. I returned to town again at 4.00 and found Weil's crowded with Fingoes and Zambesians, with no consciousness of the fact that the town store had closed its doors last night,[54] and that they could get no more food. They are only too anxious to avail themselves of the opportunity of going over to Kanya, as offered by the authorities. They were worrying me, and waiting for me to give them passes, when one of them fell in the courtyard of starvation – the poor fellow was taken to the hospital, where he died afterwards.

## Thursday, 22nd

One of the greatest troubles I have endured during the Siege is that I have been put on rations. Thus food becomes one of the greatest desires of a man's dreams, on it he would spend all his money if he could.[55]

Today I am simply going to fetch the newspaper and receive my weeks supply without any fuss. It consists of $7 \times 1$ lb tins of preserved meat, 1 lb of sugar, half a pound of tea, $\frac{1}{2}$ lb of coffee, some salt, pepper, rice, meal etc. The greatest care is exercised that one should get as little as possible of everything.

It was urgently suggested that surpluses be held for the starving people to eat, but it was this day discovered that there was sufficient oatmeal to keep them going and undesirable foodstuff has not yet been introduced. We hope it will never be. In town the thing is being done already.

The big gun has been shifted from its position west of the Stadt, and is now in its southernly place, as near as the Malmani road. It has, however, not fired a single shot today. This is only the third holiday that 'Au Sanna' has given us since her arrival. I have not mentioned that Sgt. Major Looney, of the garrison, was taken in on the 7th instant. He was tried[56] last Saturday by Court Martial, which I witnessed for the first time. Major Godley was presiding, and all the others present were dressed in their best uniforms. The court was crowded, and I left it still in progress. Sentence was deferred until today. Looney was arraigned on the Market Square and sentence was promulgated by Major Godley.[57] According to the newspaper on Tuesday, we were allowed to be present at the promulgation. He was sentenced to be reduced from the ranks of His Majesty's Service and to serve five years penal servitude. The securities[58] turned round and dismissed him, and he was handed over to the Civil Powers. I felt so sorry for him – such a pretty young fellow. I understand that he has a wife and a child. His face is exactly like Mamasinoke's.[59] He is a white Ralisa. Lovely rains fell in the night.

### Friday, 23rd

The big gun discharged seven shots during the morning. She was trying to hit a number of cattle that were grazing to the north of the town, but did not hit any.

About 100 Boers were seen to go north during the day. The whole of the day was very quiet. A fair, still and cloudy evening. No 'bad-night shot' this evening.

### Saturday, 24th

It was raining all night through. The morning in consequence is very lovely. It has been abnormally quiet all these days. But today was extraordinary. We could see early this morning that the weather would keep the Boers quiet and that was really the case. Fine soaking rains were the order of the day. Mausering and shelling were absent and the warning bell for the firing of the big gun was conspicuous in its silence. It was quite a holiday and many of us during our movements quite forgot the big gun's presence.

### Sunday, 25th

The veldt looks quite green and lovely after yesterday's rains. I have not mentioned that during the week Snyman wrote to say that he was notifying us for the last time with regard to the Sunday as he sees that as far from worshipping God we use it as a day of building forts, chopping wood and sending out 'maids' and children with passes signed by 'den Heer Belle',[60] who was formerly or still [is] magistrate of Mafeking and who at one time was refused by Kapitein Wessels well-knowing that Baden-Powell was the head official – and other such rubbish.[61] (I wonder if he means that Mr Bell should not sign passes, but should leave that duty to the O.C.) Therefore anyone showing himself on this day, or cattle going beyond their week day's grazing lines, and officers reconnoitring too far will be fired on by his Burghers.

In the morning there were several shots, and there was some Mausering to show us that Snyman was true to his word. But towards the middle of the morning all was just as calm as usual.

Runners came in from the north. They brought bad news. We are anxiously awaiting the Relief of Ladysmith and Kimberley.[62] As the last *Mail* stated General Roberts was going to the front,[63] we are expecting an account and result of his trip with big eyes. Wires came from Bulawayo to say that the telegraph between Salisbury and Beira was out of order and that is the reason why there is no news worth recording. Two Dutchmen escaped from here and went to the Boers during the day. They think their side is going to be victorious but as the Relief of the above-mentioned towns is expected shortly, they have just left in good time to discover their folly. A Native from the Boers states that Snyman had been away up north when the big gun was turned around to the west, and he ordered its return.

### Monday, 26th

A spy returned from Lothlakane this morning. He brought good news. Kimberley had been relieved during the second week in February and the line is being constructed north of Kimberley. This news, it appears, was brought to Rietfontein by a young fellow who left this place with Cronje's Commandos, and he states that Cronje was shot through the shoulders when the Relief of Kimberley was effected. Poor fellow. We will get Transvaal for Major-Genl. Lord Methuen's wounds. I wonder what the Boers are going to get for his shoulders.[64]

*Tuesday, 27th*

On horseback all day, gathering people together and arranging for their exodus tonight.[65]

A letter was sent to Genl. Snyman telling him to (1) remove all of the armed Natives away from Mafeking; (2) Restore Saane[66] back to his people at Molimola, failing which he should consider the old agreement – that Natives should take no part in the fight – at an end: Bathoen, Pula, Sechele, Ikaneng, Lenchwe, Kgama (all of the Protectorate Chiefs) would be permitted to enter the Transvaal and loot farms at random. This would be a grand affaire for even the Bahurutshe[67] would not sit still. This would be the Dutch people's final crush – at least round here. They had enough to do with Colonels Plumer and Baden-Powell, when they each had about 1,000 men. Just now they must be considered to be in a dilemma as to how they should oppose these two heads[68] – and what more if all these chiefs who are all more or less dreaded by Marico Boers should reinforce them? 'Humanity will shudder', to use Jabavu's[69] phrase.

At 4 p.m. there were about 400 men and women gathered near the Railway Bridge and more were arriving by scores.

At 6 p.m. there were about 900 of them. A waggon load of mule flesh arrived and each received a piece. At 7.00 it was discovered, after a second load had arrived, that there was not yet sufficient meat for the crowd.

I saw horseflesh for the first time being treated as human foodstuff. It looked like meat with nothing unusual about it, but when they went to the slaughter-pole for the third time and found that there was no more meat left and brought the heads and feet, I was moved to see their long ears and bold heads, and those were the things the people are to feed on. The recipients, however, were all very pleased to get these heads and they ate them nearly raw. After 7 they began to move in the direction of the B.S.A. Camp. The Civil Commissioner, who arrived on the scene half an hour earlier, looked like their Moses, and Private (now Sergeant) Abrams C.P.,[70] their Aaron. The latter is in charge of the Stadt Guard. He had been with the Barolongs since the commencement of the wars and the bravery which characterised him has distinguished him before his officers and gained for him a profound respect before all Barolongs. When one of them feels hungry and re-members that his hunger is a part of the Siege, he generally gets disgusted at the English way of going to work, which involves the prolongation of the trouble, and exclaims that there are only 2 good and brave Englishmen in this world – and they are Balofete (Lt. Colonel Walford) and Aberamo.

When this matter was got up it was directed that Sgt. Abrams and 12 of his men should accompany these people only as guides to show them the way and urge them on. Two detachments of the Protectorate Regiment were to keep their right and left flanks and do all the firing in case any Boer fires at them. We passed the B.S.A. Camp, went on to Fort Cardigan and further on past Fort Miller [71] – places which I and Mr Bell have never been – not even on a Sunday – since the commencement of the Siege, and still there was no sign of the Volunteers. We went along until we found only the O.C. and two or three other officers – but no volunteers. It is doubtful if there ever was an Exodus so momentous as the one on the day on which Israel came out of Egypt: the house of Jacob from people of a strange language; when Judah was his Sanctuary and Israel his dominion. But if brother Moses was in Mafeking this evening he would himself admit that these people's exodus gave more work or thought, considering that they are flying from a common enemy, starvation, and they do not expect to travel 3 miles before being fired on by another enemy – the Boers. The Israelites, for instance, when they left Pharaoston [72] (Kharthoum, Cairo or wherever it was) were driven out by the enemy with the approval of everyone in authority. But this unfortunate 900 we want to get rid of, and that is why we are sending them away to Canaan where we have 'milk and honey', green makatane [73] etc. which are really milk and honey compared with the mule flesh in store for them; but we have not consulted the Boers who are at present in authority and [who] will surely have things quite their own way. This disadvantage the Moses–Aaron crew did not have. (Their provisions were lamb, veal, and no horse-flesh.) [74]

When a start was made from the river, there arose cries of 'Mma, Mma'; children shouting after their mothers, and women after their children in the dark: but after passing the B.S.A. Camp, besides the heavy treads of twice 900 feet, there reigned a dead silence.

After our return we waited and heard a few Mauser volleys in the direction in which they went. I did not wait till I turned in, for at about 11.30 Matshenko knocked at the door (every inmate of the Shankaan [75] had joined the exodus) and told me that all that elaborate arrangement had burlesqued. The volunteers failed to turn up and 12 men being unable to very well fight and drive 900 people at the same time, the Boers scattered the whole crowd in every direction. This was a serious blow to me particularly taking into consideration that I have been on horseback from early till late during the last 2 days – and all that for 'niks'. [76] I turned in at 12.00, took a short nap, then heard Taelo waking me with the statement that the Barolongs are now going to take them out and I should accompany them – a perfect nuisance.

It was decided to bring them back and keep them in the hollow at Maphachwe [77] until the next evening when they will be taken out by

Natives. They were guarded all night by armed men and were not permitted to return to the Stadt.

This is a matter of such a sweeping importance as puts all other questions in the dark.

## Wednesday, 28th [78]

It has at last been resolved that Barolongs should attack down [at] the trenches by night. We spent much of the day with them there. 6 men reported themselves as having come from the Boers. They left home on Monday night. They were fired at by the Boers who eventually got them, and told them to return to Mafeking and leave in broad daylight if they wish to save their lives. They appear quite confident of getting back there if they were allowed to have it their way and it was resolved to [let them] do so in the morning. Mr Bell's horse is still gone.[79]

EDITORIAL NOTE

The month of February was not distinguished by great events or outstanding deeds. It is perhaps true that from the British point of view the month ended with a slight military credit-balance: Fort Cronje, which lay a mile to the south of the *stadt* and had formerly been an important Boer sniping-post, was captured. Apart from partially solving the persistent problem of inadequate grazing-land, this also reduced the effectiveness of Boer positions on the southern front. It brought the meagre British artillery to within range of Jackal Tree and other near-by fortifications. But the problems of physical hardship and boredom were growing more acute. A resolute front continued to be shown to a world which watched but could not see.

The townspeople only now began to experience what the Barolong had known the month before. Horseflesh began to feature regularly on the family menu. In the *stadt* malnutrition diseases (and, on occasion, fatalities) were spreading amongst the people, as is evidenced by the decision to evacuate refugees to Kanye.

The news of the Relief of Kimberley at the end of the month could not have come at a better time for beleaguered Mafeking. It was followed by a significant leap in the *Thermometer of Hope* as relief became a more immediate possibility.

The various siege-journals stress the fact that community organisation continued to improve, that the defensive system was becoming more and more difficult to breach and that both the civilian and the military populations were determined to retain a high level of morale. One suspects, however, that these were written with a knowledge that history was in the making. Patriotic 'heroism', expressed in optimistic statements, obscures the essential point which may be adduced from

126

Plaatje's February entries: that, behind the resolute front, hunger and fear were becoming potent enemies. General Snyman's policy was at last having noticeable effect.

## CHAPTER NOTES

1 The diarist's stallion. Plaatje took a keen interest in horses and continually expressed the fear (later realised) that hunger would force the general population of Mafeking to eat horseflesh.

2 Or Basotho. Oral legend has it that this group of Basotho migrated to the Mafeking District in the time of Montshiwa 1 (1849–96). They were allotted land on the fringe of the *stadt*.

3 Pitsane, now a Barolong boo Ratlou village, lies approximately forty miles west-north-west of Mafeking, on the Molopo river. It should not be confused with Pitsane (formerly spelt Pitsani) in Botswana, from which the Jameson Raid was mounted. Plaatje's figure (48) may represent the mileage of the route taken.

4 Old Kraaipan, thirty-eight miles south-east of Mafeking, is situated in what is today the Setlagole Bantu Reserve.

5 The paragraph was subject to much overwritten addition, all of which has been included here.

6 The Boers were well aware of the vital contribution made by Barolong cattle-raiders to the waning food-stocks in Mafeking. Further, the herds so frequently raided were an important source of sustenance for the besiegers themselves. Consequently, they attempted to place them as far behind their own line as logistics permitted.

7 Dutch; 'cattle-byre'.

8 Tswana: literally, 'Get out! Get out. They [the cattle] belong to [are of] Morolong [i.e., the Barolong chief]. Now they do not belong to the Boers!' These words were shouted by the raiders at the herders [presumably Rapulana-Barolong employed by the Boers]. The word *ele* in the final sentence is slightly puzzling; it implies a relative construction [literal translation: 'Now they [the cattle] do not belong, they [the cattle] of the Boers']. Liberty to translate the sentence more freely has been taken.

9 Xhosa: 'the self', 'personality', 'individuality', 'body', 'substance'. Zulu: 'root', 'basis', 'charm against evil', 'badge of bravery'. Plaatje probably chose this word to convey a wide range of meaning clustering around the notion of individuality/personality.

10 That this was not usually the case, even as regards these risky raids, is amply illustrated in the diary. Plaatje appears to have been put into a pessimistic mood by the coincidence of unfortunate occurrences.

11 A corruption of the Dutch *pelsjas* – 'fur skin jacket', which article was believed, if specially made for the purpose by an African ritual expert, to protect the wearer from harm. It is possible that Plaatje, an ardent Christian, is using the Dutch to emphasise the humour of the situation: Boers, a profoundly religious population, obtain charmed skin-jackets (from 'natives' who are characterised by them as being superstitious non-Christians) for magical protection which are then thought to help the *wearers* in a confrontation with Barolong. (It should be added that this stereotype of the superstitious Boer is still current among Barolong.)

12 Field-cornet.

13 M.D. here refers not to a Western medical doctor but a traditional priest-doctor. The Tswana term for the latter – ngaka – has been extended, since contact, to mean the former as well, so that there is no linguistic differentiation between the two. Plaatje introduces this into English by using M.D. to refer to a priest-doctor. This is a continuation of the *peljase* incident; the humour of the inversion is patent, especially in the light of the rest of the sentence.

14 Dutch: 'bone out of the foot of an ox or a horse'; more specifically a 'witch-doctor's divination-bone' (in Sotho-Tswana *ditaola*). Traditionally, knowledge of their use was a carefully protected secret.

15 Plaatje, besides working as interpreter and clerk for the Civil Commissioner, apparently acted also as unofficial administrator of the latter's organisation of African welfare during the siege.

16 This figure is probably reasonably accurate. Plaatje was involved in organising a *stadt* census, completed on 22 March 1900, which registered 5,448 inhabitants. Plaatje then calculated that half the population of the *stadt* must have left since the commencement of the siege: the African population was being encouraged to leave and seek refuge with allies elsewhere as supplies were on the wane. The first mention of an organised exodus was on 27 February, so that at this time, with emigration occurring in a haphazard manner, the figure of 7,000 is quite probable.

17 This was a stronghold to the north-west of Godley's western headquarters, its summit dominating his advanced positions. It was armed with a seven-pounder.

18 The name of his horse.

19 Plaatje persistently uses the phrase 'narrow escapade' instead of 'narrow escape'.

20 'At Crocodile Pools Colonel Plumer is opposed by the Boers entrenched in a strong position; our force is equally strongly posted, and has already caused the enemy serious losses with its shell fire. More men and guns are come to reinforce it, and it will then proceed to run the Boers out.' (*Mafeking Mail*, 8 February 1900).

21 'From 7th inst. inclusive all employers of Native Labour will be required to take out a Pass for each Native employed by them. The Pass can be obtained between the hours of 10.30 a.m. and 1 p.m. at the Resident Magistrate's Office, and that official will keep a Register of all those issued. Passes will be shown when required by military or civil authorities and any Native found in the town without a Pass will be liable to be punished by the Court of Summary Jurisdiction.' (*Mafeking Mail*, 6 February 1900).

'. . . the term Native Servants applies to all Natives in the employ of persons living in the town . . . the term Native applies to Bechuanas, Matabeles, and all those belonging to original tribes of this country. . . . Natives belonging to enrolled Native Contingents, who may desire to visit the town, should obtain a Pass from the Officer commanding the Corps. . . . Native labourers in the employ of the Government will be engaged in the Stadt by one of the Overseers. . . . The men will be brought up to the town in charge of the Overseer, who will be held responsible for seeing that the men leave the town as soon as they are paid.'

Signed E. H. Cecil (Major); 'Chief Staff Officer'.
(*Mafeking Mail*, 8 February 1900)

22 All attempts to trace this document have failed.

23 This paragraph is written in shorthand in the diary, and there is evidence that

its use here is the result of the diarist being in considerable haste. (There are numerous corrections and deletions.)

24 Existing supplies of conventional foodstuffs were calculated to last in the *stadt* until the end of March. Horses were indeed eaten thereafter, though we will never know of what Plaatje's diet consisted after his last diary entry.

25 Attempts to trace this reference have failed.

26 Dutch: 'Gentle Annie' was probably the Dutch pom-pom. No description of her size is available in the literature.

27 Plaatje's wife and son. ('Sainty' is an abbreviation for 'St Leger'. 'Free State' refers to the Orange Free State, where they were at the time.)

28 I.e., the runners.

29 Tswana: 'jump to', 'jump into'. (Sotho: 'jump to', 'exaggerate'.) This verb is written in the applicative form.

30 A popular Barolong siege-hero, this man was a cattle-raider whose boldness and bravery are still recalled by the older generation today.

31 Bathoen I, chief of the Bangwaketse at Kanye.

32 Mr James Dall, Mafeking Town Councillor, died on this day.

33 Dutch: 'bad', 'poor'.

34 Dutch: 'Council'.

35 This sentence is incomplete in the diary.

36 This refers to the annexation of British Bechuanaland to the Cape Colony, in 1895.

37 I.e., charged.

38 I.e., highly inflammable.

39 Perhaps a piece of phosphorous. It is possible that this was used in incendiaries at the time.

40 I.e., those brought in by Mathakgong on the 11th.

41 This is a surprising statement, as meat in Mafeking was now scarce. There is no other reference to the incident, although thanks are offered to Mathakgong in the *Mafeking Mail* of 16 February, for the 'succulent, juicy, undercut' that appeared on 'certain breakfast tables'.

42 Written in margin: 'The Big [Gun] round to the west now. It sent several shells into the Stadt. One burst onto one of Wessels houses. Killed one woman and wounded 3. The gun going to the far end of the garrison is a clear proof the Boers are masters of the situation.'

43 The diarist may be suggesting that his family had moved to the Eastern Cape. It is more likely that he intends 'the province to the east of here' (i.e. the Orange Free State).

44 A girl of fourteen years, she was the daughter of Lekoko and Mafikeng. Emang served as a young housekeeper for Plaatje for a period during the siege, and is still alive at the time of writing.

45 Cf. the entry of 30 December.

46 I.e., the youngsters.

47 This entry is in shorthand and gives evidence of much haste, although it is clear and decipherable.

48 This refers to Friday, 16 February.

49 This entry is written in shorthand.

50 Tributary of the Orange River with its source in the Orange Free State. At the time, this was the British 'front'.

51 Sotho-Tswana: 'When it is not for a person to cry out [call], God calls.' The comma is an editorial insertion. This may be interpreted in one of two ways. Either Plaatje is saying that when a person is powerless God comes to his aid (which makes sense in terms of the sentences that come before and after), or

he is suggesting a Job-like resignation to God's actions.

52 In the margin alongside this entry is written: 'One of the runners was wounded when they were crossing the enemy's lines from the south this morning.'

53 The entries for 21 and 22 February are written in shorthand.

54 See entry for Saturday, 10 February.

55 Food was, by this time, the major preoccupation of all. Compare Plaatje's remarks with the entry in the diary of Major F. D. Baillie (*Mafeking*) for 19 February: 'We went out to try and shoot plover, which form an acceptable addition to our rations, as we have now come down to horse-flesh and six ounces of bread per day.'

56 Sergeant-Major Looney was accused of selling government supplies.

57 The diarist wrote 'Looney', obviously in error. The text has been corrected here.

58 It is not clear what Plaatje intends here. Perhaps he is referring to the military authorities.

59 Probably: 'like Mamasinoke's (son) Ralisa'.

60 Dutch: 'The Esquire Bell', although clumsy, is perhaps the closest possible translation.

61 The *Mafeking Mail* of 17 February refers to Snyman's letters as having arrived 'a few days ago'.

62 Kimberley had actually been relieved on 15 February; but Ladysmith was not to be relieved until 28 February. News of this did not reach Mafeking until early March.

63 *Mafeking Mail*, 25 February: 'Lord Roberts has arrived in South Africa with Lord Kitchener as his Chief Staff Officer, and reinforcements are daily arriving.'

64 In the margin across this and the following entry Plaatje has written: 'I don't think I have mentioned that the Lothlakane people took up arms against us.'

65 I.e., in terms of the strategy mentioned in the entry for 10 February, Africans were encouraged to leave Mafeking for Kanye, in an attempt to make food-resources go as far as possible. Plaatje was instrumental in organising this.

66 Saane was headman of the village of Molimola. He had a distinguished record for assisting Mafeking's runners and cattle-raiders from the outside. Apparently he had been withheld from entering his village by the Boers. The British regarded this, somewhat paradoxically, as an infringement of the agreement on native neutrality, informally entered into at the start of the siege.

67 Genealogically the most senior of the Tswana tribes, the Hurutshe are thought of by Barolong as an unduly passive people.

68 Colonel Plumer's regiment initially took up a position at Tuli (on the Limpopo) to defend Rhodesia. He had commenced moving southwards, however, and was at this time occupying both Kanye and Crocodile Pools.

69 Tengo Jabavu was a well-known African editor, and in King William's Town he founded *Imvo*, the second newspaper ever published in a Bantu vernacular in South Africa. Later he and Plaatje came into conflict over the former's support of the Natives' Land Act of 1913.

70 Correctly: Abrahams, Cape Police.

71 Situated north-west of the town, en route to Kanye.

72 An interesting title, considering subsequent South African history.

73 Sing., *lekatane*. Tswana: 'Kaffir melons', 'vegetable marrows' (Brown, *Secwana-English Dictionary*, 1931). Sotho: 'large species of bitter melon', 'Kaffir melons' (Kriel, *New English-Sesotho Dictionary*, 1958). Among Barolong it refers only to melons, not marrows.

74 The words 'were lamb, veal, and no horseflesh' were written in shorthand.

75 Presumably the area of the Shangaan encampment.

76 Dutch: 'nothing'.

77 Probably 'Hidden Hollow' (along the Molopo, west of the Stadt); local Barolong no longer recall the name.
78 This and the following entry are in shorthand.
79 This is the first allusion to the matter in the diary.

# 5 March 1900

## Thursday, 1st

A fine cloudy morning. Just remembered that I am now commencing my seventh year in the service.[1] This has been the busiest week I have had since the Siege [began]. Thirty of the Refugees were sent out this morning. They went right up to Game Tree where the Boers received them, it appeared, quite cheerfully.

## Friday, 2nd

We are still very busy with the food matter. It is proposed to erect a place in the Stadt where soup will be cooked for the benefit of the poor. It is soup made of oatmeal and horseflesh and as there are a great many hungry people in the place they each receive a good feed gratis.

The big gun pumped in a lot of shells in the morning, but as it was raining during the day, shooting was consequently very mild.

I heard in the afternoon that 'Au Sanna' had been taken to the parapet.[2] They are probably moving her somewhere else. In the evening at about 8.00, our Nordenfeld started bombing and kept up his patter incessantly. One could simply conclude that someone saw them putting the big gun up somewhere in the vicinity. It was very grand to listen to Master Nordenfeld's 'ptions – ptions – ptions'. We have not heard it for a long time.

## Saturday, 3rd

Early this morning 'Au Sanna' opened fire on the Brickfields. She is back at her old position opposite the Nordenfeld's, across the Makane valley and therefore miserably close to the Brickfields. By 7 o'clock she had already put in 41 shells and then [3] 'shut up' after wounding Sgt.-Major Taylor and two others so severely that he is not expected to live. Taylor's case is pretty sad for he was one of the best men we had in the place.[4] He worked his way quietly to the Brickfields until he took his position after killing a considerable number of Boers. It was only last week that he told me that if he knew that 'such conditions' were awaiting him in Mafeking, he would never have come up here.

One of 'Au Sanna's' gunners was shot today and he died on the spot.

Two more were wounded at the Brickfields and another of the Bechuanaland Rifles. These are all we ourselves saw and there are probably
many more. The range of our big guns appears very effective. (The
above-mentioned were killed by Maxims.) They have taken off the Big
Gun again and we wonder where it has gone this time. This has been an
unfortunate day for Boer, British, etc. The Sidzumos lost cattle very
heavily – 14 all told. Eight killed and six wounded. One poor brute's
nose was completely ripped off. It was a mess and I had often drunk her
milk.

The Commissioner's Department bought the whole lot. Old Sidzumo
wanted to have cattle at the end of the war, but was told that that is an
impossibility.

### Sunday, 4th

This was another unfortunate day.[5] Sgt.-Major Bill (Colonial Contingent) was wounded on the arm and a Morolong Scout attached to
the C.P.[6] was shot through the neck. These things occurred at the
Brickfields. It being Sunday, they walked out of their trenches and
exposed themselves, and that is how they were shot. The Boers must
be getting some nasty knocks somewhere for they now don't care a hang
about worshipping their God on Sundays. The rattling of Mausers today
was just as brisk as on ordinary weekdays. I went to town and also to
Maphacoe[7] where I found a little boy who had been out eating
moretlwa[8] with two others. They were fired on by the Game Tree Boers
who wounded him[9] through both thighs and one arm. He could not say
what became of the other two. Rumours came in and confirmed the
news about the Relief of Kimberley and also that our friend Cronje is in
a tight fix at Jacobsdal[10] and the Troops expect to catch him. Some
Boers up north have retired before Colonel Plumer at the Crocodile
Pools.

### Monday, 5th [11]

The Big Gun is said to be back. It is near MacMullen's. There was
some very brisk volleying in the direction of the Brickfields, and we
hear that the 'Kaapenaars'[12] have vacated their position there. Captains
FitzClarence and Williams, with several men, rushed the place, and
took it, minus any casualties. Poor Taylor died during the day. Few
people who have not been in Mafeking during the raid, will understand
how valuable his services have been to the Garrison. He had been as
plucky a soldier of His Majesty's during the Siege as he has been the
lowly servant of Christ in the English Church in times of peace. He
was part of the Military Force, and his funeral is to be attended by the
Officer Commanding, and other Officers of the Garrison.

A man left here on Saturday last for Kanya. He was fallen upon by the Boers, who, on catching him, sent him back to Mafeking. The Natives had been disarmed, they told him, and were going back to their homes.[13] The Boers were also going to leave the place, and camp at the border. He saw them actually loading up, and the preparations clearly indicated that they were going to leave. This has still to be proved, although we could not altogether disbelieve him, as these Boers have surely not come here for life.

## Tuesday, 6th

A beautiful morning. 'Au Sanna' was silent all the morning, and only opened fire effectively at 4.00 p.m. Many people were taken in when they saw the dummy gun,[14] and no 'Sanna'. Last week we made them waste a waggon-load of shells by pressing the dummy truck on the long disused railway line, near Mr B. W.[15] I saw the chimney-pipe sticking out of it, so that it looked like the armoured train. Sometimes a 'Guy Fawkes' is constructed outside one of the trenches and made to jump about by means of strings fixed to him, as this would draw out showers of Mauser ammunition. We will do anything to remind the Boers of the dynamite trick of the 13th October, and we have done a lot of harm to the Boers with this sort of thing.

'Au Sanna' let off two shots during the day; punctually at 4.00 and 6.00 p.m. respectively.

## Wednesday, 7th

A very quiet day. The bells rang twice, but 'Au Sanna' never fired.

## Thursday, 8th

Very good news in this morning by runners from the north and messengers from Saane's.[16]

| Boers | Recapture of Colesberg |
| bolted | Dordrecht taken at the point of bayonets. |
| before | |
| Buller | |

Glorious slaughter of Women Slayers.[17]

Brilliant onslaught on women murderers.[18]

Cronje's term as 'general'[19] is at its final stage – 1,000 Boers killed around him and 7,000 taken prisoner with him.

Mathakgong and his band are coming tonight with a hundred beautiful cattle they espied near Maritzani.

Snyman disarmed the Rietfontein Rebels[20] who now wonder where they'll go. Malan has retired in front of Colonel Plumer who is at Lobatsi[21] and Snyman leave Mafeking with Malan tomorrow.

'Au Sanna' let off once, at 8 this morning.

*Friday, 9th*

'Au Sanna' never let off a shot today. It may [be] because they are short of ammunition or that, their gunner being shot, no one is able to control the gun.

Some women went out in the direction of Signal Hill to gather green makatane, etc. from their fields. They saw a few young Boers who told them to glean in haste and return before their parents come as they will not permit them to take away any. Mathakgong has not turned up yet.

*Saturday, 10th*

'Sanna' fired two shots in the morning. Nothing eventful. The horse thieves sentenced.[22]

*Sunday, 11th*

Mathakgong came in this morning. Since they left here they spent the week very close to Madibe Siding.[23] During the week they sent six men to a neighbouring farm to steal some goats. Four men came back with a sheep in the evening, the fifth turned up next morning, and the sixth failed to put in an appearance until they left their camp. On Friday they saw a mounted man coming past their camp, with a packet of dynamite in his hand. He left his horse, then walked towards the railway line. One man wanted to shoot him as he bent over the line, but the others refused as he was unarmed. How unlike the Boers, who would shoot any one of us without hesitating to find out if he was armed. After this they heard a loud explosion and the man did this a second and third time. He was blowing up the line. When he returned they recognised him as old 'Burwise' of the farm Rooidammetjies.[24] It was at once resolved that his cattle should be taken.

On Saturday evening they attacked his farm, drove the Boers, servants, dogs, etc. out of the homestead and then took the cattle. They wanted to get hold of the calves but when they opened the kraal (during the heat of the fire) the calves jumped out at the back and followed their running owners.

Three horses that were tied there also did the same and they only came away with the cattle – 27 fat animals. The journey was uneventful. They had intended to cross the Boer lines a little to the east of the old railway line but by mistake they came too high and were surprised to find themselves at the Jackal Tree Boer Fort, where the Boers opened fire on them. Mathakgong shouted at the top of his voice:

'Likganela re li loele. Ba tshega bare re basimane ba likoalo ba ba senang go iphemela. Maburu a, ebile Manyesemane a ba lamalitse ka go ba neela fela yaka ba rata lieme re li loele.'[25] On hearing this one of the Boers mounted a grey horse and swifted off towards their western fort shouting for reinforcements. But the battle was already on then. They fought their way through and lost one man, killed – poor Maiku was a very plucky fellow. He left here in December at a time when we knew nothing of what goes on in Kimberley and he reached Kimberley, returned, and brought us news about the true state of affairs there. The Boers killed one ox. Our men killed two Boers that they saw, and heard one screaming some distance to the left. He screamed for a long time – till our men had left Jackal Tree far behind. Things are getting very strained now. People cannot get any cattle without having to risk very much. Another party went out last night and Teacher Potiphao is going out tonight with 24 men. He has since the beginning performed brilliant services and has always taken a part in whatever act the Barolongs distinguished themselves with during the Siege. We hope he will do as well in the veldt.[26]

## Monday, 12th

Paul [27] took 50 men and attacked a Dutch fort about three miles to the south of the Stadt last night. As they were leaving they sent a man to Captn. Marsh [28] for ammunition but he came back saying Captn. Marsh was not there so they had to go and attack the place with about 3 to 7 rounds of ammunition per man. Fortunately they went round and reached the further end of the trench unobserved until they opened fire on the sleeping Boers. There was a sudden scramble for the wall, but numbers of them were knocked down by bullets while in the act of climbing over the fence. The battle was very successful and just at the time they would have taken the fort they were obliged to leave it on account of their ammunition being all spent. They are certain of eight killed Boers besides the lot that were screaming and groaning in the fort.

'Au Sanna' went for us during the morning, probably endeavouring to shell their cattle out of us. The cannon has been very quiet all last week and this sudden waking up is very undesirable as we have already got unused to it.

Two cattle looting parties are still at large and we hope if they are as successful as Mathakgong we will frighten the Boers away from here as they will fancy that the whole of their country is simply swarming with armed Natives.

Women are now always going out to Moleloane [29] and coming home with a lot of melons and Kaffircorn, so we are wondering why the Boers permit them to get out so far while they have not previously even been allowing them to go out to get some bushes for fuel behind the Convent on Sundays. Some of the women get driven back but go round to try somewhere else and come back successful.

## Tuesday, 13th

More news – all of it good. Ladysmith [30] has been relieved by General Sir R. Buller, who although he lost somewhat heavily, killed 2,000 Boers and took 3,000 prisoners. Some of our cattle raiders came back. Their trip was interesting though accompanied by misfortunes, and they had a warm time of it yesterday. After leaving Mafeking, 'Luiku' and the northerner Colbourne Msikuiya,[31] could not agree with the majority of the party, and he turned towards Polfontein [32] with the royal following of 6 all told. 18 men went towards Madibe and the following were their adventures: during the middle of the morning they saw 11 Boers riding all along their spoor towards the koppie on which they were sheltered. They hid rightly behind some stones until the Boers came on the koppie. One of the Boers saw them. They exchanged fire and the Boers ran away leaving one man and a horse killed.

They know the Boers would go for reinforcements, so they decided they should go to a hole in the open plain round Madibe Siding. Entrenched in a hole they would, of course, have the Boers at their mercy as there is absolutely nothing behind which to take cover. They refreshed themselves with some sweetcakes, and watermelons they had gathered in the field, then made for this hole. The Boers returned at noon; 16 of them, all mounted, with spare horses carrying ammunition. The Boers came riding carelessly along their spoor, but our fellows sat tight until their leader, when within 40 yards of the hole, saw them and said: 'Hier's de Kaffirs.'[33] A man hit him on the breast and knocked him down. He fired, while [he] was on the ground, wounding one of our chaps on the buttocks before another hit him on the forehead. After this our fellows had a brief but very hot battle. The Boers ran away leaving 6 dead men and 5 horses on the field. 2 horses were taken alive, with their saddles, bridles, etc. by our fellows; also 2 rifles and bandoliers belonging to the dead Boers. From here our men came homeward. They put the wounded man on one of the horses and came all along the railway line. The Boers accompanied them from a distance of between 800 and 1,000 yards, sniping [at] them all the time. They continued this until they reached Ga-Koi-Koi (4 miles from here) then thought it advisable to go back again as it was too early to come into Mafeking. They did so and the Boers accompanied [them] back again to Madibe where they waited until it was late enough to cross the Boer lines and get into Mafeking under cover of the dark. When they left Madibe the Boers left them for good and went to fetch their dead. Their horses are a beautiful grey gelding with a first class saddle, and a big mare. The bridles and the other saddle are third hand. The 2 rifles are a splendid pair of Martini's 'Made especially for the Z.A.R. by Wesley Richards'. This was stamped very neatly: 'J. J. Jonck, Z.A.R. 1900' within a circle.

Our losses were: one man, wounded at the fight, and one man wounded slightly during the march, at long range. The enemies' losses were one man and his horse, killed at the koppie, 6 Boers and 5 horses, killed during the fight, one man and one horse killed while our fellows were coming down along the hill, and 2 horses taken away alive. We wonder how many wounded.

'Au Sanna' is very hot now, like yesterday. She gave us thunder and lightning all day. She, however, did no damage during the day, but her last shell this evening did considerable damage and also struck a place that had never been struck before – the Court House. At 5.00 p.m. there are always a number of people congregated in the yard to fall in [for] their night's duty, get pay, etc., etc. The soup kitchen is close by and as soup is issued in the afternoon there are hundreds of Natives always gathered there. The shell came round at 6.15, flew over the roof and abruptly dropped over the chimney into what at one time was the C.C. and R.M.'s [34] Private Office, and made a terrible wreck of everything inside: the partitions, walls, chairs, books, tables, etc.; but the greatest of all mysteries is how the shell went [on] to bag the people outside, amputated legs, shattered bodies and heads to the number of 8 killed and wounded – a doleful procedure.

### Wednesday, 14th

'Au Sanna' is still as hot as ever. We have heard this morning about 'Relief of Ladysmith' in duplicated dispatches from the north. The originals have been caught by the Boers evidently, for bearers state that the runners who preceded them have been caught.

A lot of women are always going out to their fields at Moleloane to gather melons and fresh kaffir corn. They go right across the Boer lines. There are so few Boers in the trenches that they cannot control the multitude of women. If they tell 16 to drop their stuff 'about 60' will bring in theirs from somewhere else. This shows that the Boer trenches are quite empty and 're tshosiwa ka merora fela'.[35] They have all gone north to oppose Plumer. That is why Natives [36] are guarding now.

### Thursday, 15th

It rained during last night. We have rain nearly every day. Teacher Kolobe came back. His following of 5 supported him right through. They attacked a Boer Homestead on Tuesday but failed to bag the cattle as the farmers were too numerous for them. They came back via Madibe and saw the dead and wounded horses shot by the balance of his party on Monday.

They killed one Boer in the attempt to capture cattle.

I had a very narrow escape at 4 o'clock this afternoon. My first warning was but the screeching of the shell when it came straight up to me. I was riding 'Pony' round from Lookoani and turning round the curve at Letsi's [37] place. I hardly knew what to do as for 6 seconds (or thereabouts) I felt that it was coming straight to me. I have never felt so nasty as during that little period of my life, until it burst and the pieces flew overhead. The pony had already turned round about and was going backwards with me.

The result was a bloodstirring whine amongst the women folk in the house next to me. I myself was so shaken that I scarcely felt anything when I heard that it had smashed old Letsi's head and killed the poor old fellow instantly.

These narrow escapades are not only undesirable because one barely escapes death, but surely because they give one the impression that many of them are in store for one in the little future left for one; and every one of them will [be] narrower than its predecessor — until he loses a leg, arm, some limb — or even life.

Many people are leaving Mafeking at night now. They experience no difficulty in crossing the outpost and the Boer lines. We are all convinced that the Boers have considerably diminished during the past week or two.

We are very restless about the safety of the two parties of cattle raiders still at large.

I heard something very extraordinary today. The Administrator of Martial Law have authorised the municipality to levy dog tax as they want to get rid of as many dogs as possible.[38] Some unlicensed dogs were found, destroyed and buried by the Town Ranger.

Our local Zambesi friends unearthed them, immediately the ranger's assistants left the scene, and promptly cooked them for dinner, which gave the Barolong sections of the community the impression that there is more in a dog than they were ever told there was.

*Friday, 16th*

It was not so hot as we have had it from 'Sanna' since the beginning of the week.

MacKenzie has taken Jackal Tree with his 'Black Watch' of which Titshalakazi's 'Gun' [39] was a member when he got shot. They went to Jackal Tree at the beginning of the week and found no Boers there. He occupied the place but vacated it on account of it being so far away from here, and far away from any water. Last night, however, they went up there, and took shelter in the Boer trench. They saw them coming: one Boer and 3 Natives (rebels), all mounted. They came, off-saddled their horses, and laid down their rifles when our Transkeian friends coolly volleyed them, killing the Boer and a rebel, wounding one rebel, and causing the other to run away. They took their four horses with saddles, rifles, etc.

We are anxiously waiting for runners and we wonder why we receive no news.

### Saturday, 17th

We are feeling the strain a little, not because we are defeated but simply because we have received no dispatches this week.

There are some Shangaans and Zambesis – very few of them, as the majority have left this place and gone up country. They are going to be fed on soup, the 'stuff' we hear was used for white ladies in Kimberley. Here it is used by destitute people who cannot provide for themselves. It was not really a case of starvation but planned strategy on the part of the officers.[40]

### Sunday, 18th

A funny thing – we received no fewer than 8 runners today – all from the south. One left here early in December. His mate returned in the road. One left here late in December; his mate got sick and he left him halfway. 2 left here in January and they were four when they left Kimberley on the 18th. ult. 2 were sent to Setlagoli by Lady Sarah Wilson. They managed to deliver their messages in what may be termed a 'Sherlock Holmeish' sort of fashion. From there they went to Motlotli Emang's:[41] they got there simply through the doings of Providence. One afternoon, being sick, they called on what they found to be a wayside farm house for hospitality. On stating that they came from Mafeking the previous week and were requesting to be concealed against Boer discovery, they were told to go inside. They saw the children running to the fields to report to the lady what important visitors there were at the house. She came – Motlotli Emang did – sat down, gasped, sighed, then muttered in broken sentences: 'So you are from Mafeking?'

'Yes.'

'Do you know anybody named Plaatje?'

'Oh yes, he is . . .'

'Is he still alive and well?'

'Yes he is in charge of our work and if you treat us hospitably you would be obliging him.'

She heaved a big sigh of relief, then went outside, they believe, to weep with joy, for on her return she said that she had always heard that three quarters of the inhabitants of Mafeking had been killed by 'Sanna' and she was always thinking I was one of them.

Two of the runners are Mr Weil's. They left here in February for Kimberley. They were taken prisoners at Maribogo [42] and sent down to Vryburg, where they were kept as prisoners at large for some time. During that time they heard that Mr Rosenblatt was sending dispatches between Vryburg and Kimberley and handed the dispatches to him. They were buried in a furrow outside the town all this time. All of these runners have been picking each other up on the road, and just outside Mafeking they came across one party of cattle raiders and they all came in. The fellows from Kimberley say that they never expected that Kimberely would hold out up to the end.

The condition of the inhabitants was very miserable. They had no words to describe the state of the people. White ladies fleeing, babies in hand and piccaninnies all round, to the bottom of the mine [43] – tens of fathoms deep, to take cover from the shells. They never for a moment thought that the people would hold out, and they often told them that Mafeking was not half as badly off as that. When the Troops arrived it was something worth seeing. They say that we who were not there missed a very touching scene. White ladies can scream, they say, just as loud as Native women – 'Ya ba retla tlhoyana.' [44] They said they saw thousand of Boers being marched to gaol and they were surprised. They wondered how so many people could surrender to other warriors when they had their guns, ammunition and everything. They have a far greater contempt for the Boers than they ever thought they would have. Fancy surrendering to other men when you are armed. The Serolong axiom for an armed man is: 'Shoa o ikaletse'[45] i.e. even if your antagonists be a hundred, kill at least one before they catch you. They came past Pniel.[46] Rev. Westphal has been taken prisoner along with 4 men – one of them I think is Abel Pienaar. The three are Bechuanas and goodness knows who they are. Barkly has been retaken.[47] The Boers all fled from there like wild rabbits immediately at the sight of the British. It is marvellous how Rev. Westphal managed to turn traitor,[48] when he sent me that hot letter going for me for having leanings towards the Transvaal and Krugerism, simply because I sympathised with Ado Burton [49] during the last election; and he could not be convinced by my reasons that the young Q.C. earned my sympathies not because he was supported by the Afrikander Bond, but simply because he was a negrophilist and did a lot for us while I was in Kimberley. He acted on our behalf directly on the platform, in the press, and at the bar.

The effects of the war are going to be bitterer still – no matter what its results. But this is one of those things, as Lord Dundreary would say: 'No fellah can understand.'

They brought much news about the doing of the Boers outside today. The little skirmishes our people had with the Boers outside have had a great effect among the latter. It is reported that about 1,000 armed Barolongs are scattered all over the country. Two hundred of them are at Madibi and they have 2 Maxims. Mathakgong's name is a household word on every farm. The cattle have been centralised and strong guards put over them. They are strongly encamped in trenches surrounding the cattle fence, and they are just ready to give him a cordial reception. They say he has killed many Boers at their farms during last month, including women and children.

They have been informed that the Kromdraai Laager was going to be moved to the border last Friday. Goodness knows if it is true. But we wonder how the Boers can stay around here much longer when they had such a good knock at Kimberley and the Troops [50] were at the Vaal on the 20th of last month.

## Tuesday, 20th

I have been very busy officially — so busy that I have failed to jot down a note or two, and I scarcely remember what took place yesterday beyond a few notes that I consider worth recording. While at Court this morning I was practising shorthand and I find the following:

Albert pleaded not guilty to being found on the premises of Masethaisho without permission at about midnight last Saturday. The evidence showed that Complainant is a young widow and resides by herself with a little child in the hut.

An old man was called upon to give evidence. After being duly sworn, he denied all knowledge of the case. Asked what he came to town for, he answered: 'Merely for a stroll.' (The Court was held in the open air.)

Case no. 2 was an old Zulu charged with stealing some wood from the Government 'Scherm' [51] between the Hospital and Convent. Plea: 'Not guilty', as he did not know that the wood was anyone's property.

Case No. 3: 'Some-one-or-other' — theft of green mealies, the property of Samson Gape.[52]

Case No. 4: An old, miserable looking half-starved Changaan [53] was charged with theft of green mealies — the property of the chief, Lekoko. The plea: 'Guilty, under provocation — hunger.'

Case No. 5; Lucas, a Bosoanalander,[54] suspected as a spy. The prisoner, without being called upon to plead, was remanded.

Case No. 6: Willie Maretletle of B.D., a special guard at the gaol, pleaded not guilty to neglect of duty in that he did, on or about the

142

18th inst. wrongly and unlawfully permit prisoner 'Captain' to go into the gaol kitchen against orders.

Case No. 7: 'Captain', a prisoner undergoing a sentence of 9 months with hard labour, pleaded not guilty to the theft of a panni-kin of soup – prisoners' rations.

Case No. 1: Guilty. The Court came to the conclusion that the prisoners must have been aware that the Complainant was a widow who lived by herself, and that they were therefore a very serious purpose. The charge ought to have been that of attempted rape. Sentence – 36 lashes with the Cat-o'-9-tails.

Case No. 2: verdict – guilty. Sentence – that he be attached to De Kock's Corner for a period of 3 days, watching the 'Scherm' against wood thieves.

Case No. 3: verdict – guilty. Sentence – 6 days with hard labour.

Case No. 4: verdict – guilty, but prisoner being too weak and 'maar'[55] to undergo sentence – is remanded sine die.

The big 94 pounder was on very splendid terms with me this morning. The 'loading and pointing' bells rang early this morning but the gun never fired until I left home for town. I walked to Mr Stent's place in a very finicky mood, but just when I was within 20 yards of the door of his dug-out, the last bell rang; and I was just in time to take shelter. When I left Stent, the next waited till I crossed the Market Square and took shelter at Lippman's. Shell No. 3 waited until I reached the Chief Paymaster's dug-out, and from there I went to the Residency. I put the type-writer at the door of our little bomb-proof and was going to commence my work, when the bell rang again and I bobbed in. The usual row took place, there was a pause and then a loud 'xap' and bits of gravel drizzled into the dug-out. When we came out I thought my fatty little pony had followed Whiskey, for the table was simply enveloped in a cloud of dust. A short time revealed the fact that the well had been smashed; and the fact that the shell exploded right in the water is accountable for the unusually curt report of the explosion.

It rained during the afternoon. If we had as much food as rain, then things would be alright.

### Wednesday, 21st

Myself, Philemon and Mr Gates are taking a census of the Stadt. The latter and an assistant are taking [it] across the river. Phil starts at Tloung,[56] myself at Bokone, and we'll meet in the centre. It is a tedious, bothersome job. We commenced at 7.00 and at 10.00 I was knocked up.

The people are vexing me exceedingly: one would ask me what I wished to do with the name of the owner of a place, another would object to a repetition of the census as they were counted [registered] twice already during the present Siege. Another would say: 'no wonder the present, unlike all previous Sieges of Mafeking, is so intolerable for the unfortunate beleaguered people are counted like sheep.' Another would stand at the door, empty herself of the whole of her stock of bad words, then threaten me to 'just touch my pen and jot down any numbers of her family'. The so-and-so!

Another would give a cordial reception – so cordial that I would fancy [that] she will offer me a pipe full or a cigarette. She will act to my greatest satisfaction throughout in every way, except giving me the proper answer. I never knew that my store of patience was so bottomless – until the evening when I came home and found I had no fewer than 1,677 persons on my list. I have not been to town all day today – the first day for 5 months. I hear 5 miles [57] have been captured by the Cape Boys from the Boers at the Brickfields. The Kromdraai Laager is moved away from there. Two runners who were bound for Kimberley failed to leave owing to the long train of Boer waggons from Kromdraai circuiting round to the Transvaal side of the place – the first dawn of liberty.

Mathakgong left with nearly 30 men on another cattle raiding expedition – his fourth during the present siege.

I have not seen my Siege friends (the beggars) today. There were always scores of them every day at the Residency and they were relieved by the soup kitchen. They are made up of the blackish races of this continent – mostly Zulus and Zambesians. They venerate the Civil Commissioner and call me 'Ngwana's Molimo'.[58] It is really pitiful to see one who was too unfortunate to hear soon enough that there was a Residency in Mafeking, and, being too weak to work, never had a chance to steal anything during the last 6 days, and so had nothing to eat. Last month one died in the Civil Commissioner's yard. It was a miserable scene to be surrounded by about 50 hungry beings, agitating the engagement of your pity and to see one of them succumb to his agonies and fall backwards with a dead thud. Surely those Transvaal Boers are abominable. I really do not think they are children of the same Dutchland as the inhabitants of the O.F.S. No wonder their President was a judge while Oom Paul was a 'schaap-wachter'.[59]

I wonder where is Gates: my total for today is 1,677, Philemon's 734. They were getting on much worse than I. Keshupile was his 'moshupatsela'.[60] He went with him till dinner-time and then started grumbing that he did not estimate that the trouble of this work was a tenth of what it is. Tsipithata [61] is away cattle raiding.

*Thursday, 22nd*

Turned out at 7.00 and tackled the census. I reached our home on the beat at 8.40 then paused a bit for breaking fast. After this I went on [with] it again, knocked off at 12.00 for lunch; at it again at 3.00 to 4.30, when I finished it all.

| | | |
|---|---|---|
| I had | 2,597 | There are therefore no fewer than 5,448 people in the Stadt. |
| Mr Gates | 1,557 | |
| Mr Mahlelebe | 1,294 | |

This shows that about 10,000 people were in the Stadt at the commencement of hostilities, as quite half the population have been clearing out in 4's and 5's as the tension became more and more strained.

*Friday, 23rd*

We had another very quiet day. There must be some sort of a machinery resolving itself in a way decidedly unpleasant to the Boers. They have not fired a shot with their big gun – the first time for 2 days in succession. The runners who were caught came in this morning with good news.

*Saturday, 24th*

Morning dawned somewhat pleasantly. During the night the Boers were forced to leave their trenches in the Brickfields – the nearest to Mafeking – and fall 1,000 yards backwards. When our forces occupied the Dutch 'marope'[62] they suddenly remembered that the place is most certainly mined with dynamite and immediately searched and discovered the spot where the mine is, then cut the cord which the enemy was going to pull in order to cause a destructive explosion. This must have caused the Boers to wonder why the thing refused to work – but such was the case. The mine was emptied and the dynamite brought into town.

Fresh newspapers were found in the trench stating Bloemfontein had been occupied last month, and other valuable information. Also that 3 cattle raiders were caught stealing 38 head of cattle on the 17th – they were all killed and the cattle recaptured minus casualties – and similar 'rot'.

The Laager at Kromdraai is moving round. We hope all the wagons have passed today. Runners said Col. Plumer [was] at Macheng [63] the day before yesterday, making for Disaneng [64] with 500 men. Our raiders came in with some cattle and good news. We will soon be cheering. The big gun never fired again today and things looked quite pleasant. We had a sweet holiday, Tshipithata.[65]

## Sunday, 25th

No change yet is apparent. We had a very windy day, which made the Sunday somewhat unpleasant. Emang has been such an acquisition to our domestic circle that we wonder what we can do without [her]. It was, besides, a boon to her as it made her unused to the unceremonious 'squatting' and allowed her to occupy her time in cooking and doing such household practice as will fit her for greater cares in future. She already knows not only how to cook, but also how to economise with the scanty groceries and preserves everything with skill and fore-thought. She takes more pride in keeping the room and furniture tidy than in joining useless games in 'nooks and corners', as Rud Mickinya would say; but still, for all, Mafeking gives me notice that I must be pre-pared to part with her on Wednesday next. This is the worst news I have received for months. I was unable to speak to her, as I considered she took a pride in seeing her daughter learning so progressively, and the question took me by very great surprise.

We get our rations – groceries (tea, coffee, sugar, pepper, and salt), vegetables (greenmealies, beet, cabbage, turnips, carrots, etc. from the gardens and fields on the river beds) and preserved meat from a govern-ment store provided for the purpose. These we draw weekly and have to call early for them, once every week, but the bread is a nuisance for this we have to call [for] once every day, and each time one gets a little bit – not fit to keep St Leger alive more than a few hours. If the issuer likes, he can successfully cause us to do without it by telling our messenger that he was too late if he called at 7.00 in the morning, and too early if he called at 3.00 in the afternoon; and when he comes at the right time, he would tell the messenger that I should have called person-ally, well knowing that this is an impossibility.

## Monday, 26th

We had a very quiet day, there being hardly anything worth mention-ing except in the afternoon, when a 7-pounder was posted in the Brick-fields and shelled the Boer trenches. This drew all the wrath of 'Au Sanna' on the Brickfields and she went for the bricks with all the vigor and strength she can command. It was quite a novelty to hear her after the last 5 days of peacefulness. There was no danger on either side.

## Tuesday, 27th

I woke at 5.00 to find a fine peaceful morning. One could even wish that a morning like that ought to find one in a peaceful neighbourhood where one will partake of the sweet balmy air without any interference. I found I had nothing to do, so I lay down to slumber again. Just a little after 6.00 again the 9-pounder Krupp opened the ball from Game Tree.

I was wondering at [it] when it was followed by what appeared to be a 15-pounder from Jackal Tree, by 'Au Sanna', and several others. They kept it up all the morning. Every bomb-proof in the place was almost useless as shells were bursting from every direction.

It was a terrible morning.[66] When I left home I was simply bewildered and hardly knew what to do. I was intending to go up to the rocks, which I had deserted since the middle of November, for since then we never had it half so hot. Even at New Year it was terrible; but nothing resembling this. I stopped at the rocks, which are much more comfortable than a dug out, where one cannot see what goes on outside. I was wondering [if] this was going to be our future lot, or whether it was simply a one day's warming up. It is difficult to describe the scene, just as difficult as it is to tell how many guns there were against us. We are only sure of one thing, and that is that there were some big guns against us which have not been in Mafeking [before]. Since the big gun left its first position our house has always been out of its view so that it has not been in danger of being hit, but this morning they were mercilessly in our line. A fragment of shell that burst just at the Gape's dropped on the roof of the back house, but did not penetrate it. While I was going to the rocks, 'Au Sanna' was firing in such rapid succession that 3 shells burst all about me before I got there. This is to say nothing at least of the smaller fry. I screwed up as much courage as I could and left the rocks to go to the Court of S.J.[67] in town. It was something unbearable while I was walking between the town and the Stadt to see a horse being blown to smitherines; but when I reached the town I met the prisoners being marched back to gaol – the court was already over.

The by-word, of course, was 'what could be the meaning of this heavy entertainment?' It was something invigorating for me to find a man who had come from Kimberley with dispatches and had left the Troops in Vryburg.[68] This is such good news that one does not mind the heavy shelling; but still things are just as mixed up as they could be. A 12 pound shell went in through the air pipe of a dug out in which a lady and her family was sheltered, bursting inside, injuring the lady and wounding her servant girl. Sergt. Abrams, the White Morolong, got the front half of his foot knocked off while he was in the Stadt visiting a Native whose buttocks had been knocked clean off by a shell. One woman had her jaws dislocated and shattered. I took a statement from the man who saw the Troops, then lost my shorthand notes, and failed to remember what he had told me and the public did not read it till the following day.[69] Nine horses were killed that day and I wonder how many more animals. By dinner time 'Au Sanna' alone had put in 65 shells – i.e. 6110 pounds of cast iron, mortar, etc. into the place – a record in 1900. There was a brief respite at 12.00 noon during which I rode home, but it only gave me a chance to reach there. I have been subjected to shellfire everyday for 5 months, during which the Boers always had a great reverence for breakfast and dinner hours, but today they treated these two hours with very great disrespect.

We are all very sorry at Sergt. Abrams being wounded at this time. He was the father of the Barolong snipers and a very brave man. Three Natives wounded at the soup kitchen concluded the day's damage to life and property. The man who tells us about the Troops states that Bud, and several others, reached Kimberley after its relief. This is such cheerful news that one's head can hardly hold the joy; but I could nearly knock him down for not having told him that he was intending to come up here.[70] It took me some time to realise the fact that when we dispatch runners we would object to their preaching [their] intended journey from every housetop.

*Wednesday, 28th*

We had a very quiet day. Still and peaceful, [with] next to no shooting. During the morning I rode over to the location to purchase one of the horses lifted from the Boers by the Fingoes. I met the fellow in town and [he] told me that I could have the gelding for £14.10.0. I told Rojane to get a note from him, and [to] take it over to the seller's brother who would receive the money from him, and hand over the horse. Subsequently, I rode over to the location myself, and found the 'brother' (?) who, even if he had been inclined to hand over any horse, appeared to have no horse at all. I asked him to fetch it, but he said he wondered where it was. When I explained the puerility of allowing a horse to stray out of view, particularly when it is a captured horse which is likely to bolt away any minute, he appeared very seedy, but volunteered to walk about the location looking for the horse with me. He however, succeeded to polish me off by telling me that the sellers had gone to town on horseback. I demanded Rojane's note and to my utter amazement, found the wording to be as follows: 'Lendoda ifunaku tenga ihashe nge £15 kodwa u linde mna nodofika.'[71]

Shortly after this, I learnt that the horse was sold at 9 o'clock this morning. I, however, waited until the cheat's arrival and on demanding my horse, he knocked about the location from house to house inquiring if the people had not seen this horse. One little boy curtly gave him the following answer: 'Kaloku waya nalo edolopene andikange ndilibone.'[72] This fairly knocked him up and he nearly fell on his knees begging me to go home as he was sure to bring the horse at 3.30 p.m. It is 11.10 already, and no horse has turned up yet – the long and short of it was that when the spoil was divided he preferred to retain the horse. He was only entitled to £7, and, as the horse was valued at £12, he had to refund £5. The owners of the £5 were pressing him for the money, so he sold the horse this morning. The reason why he wanted to sell it over again to me may be found in exactly the same spot – that of the cause of the suit: 'Dingiswayo vs Moss.'[73] By the way, he is also a Dingiswayo.

During the afternoon I purchased a spank from Lt. MacKenzie 'Black Watch' at £16 and I immediately got a job for him.

Rojane is anxious to ride dispatches, and he is such a professional horseman that he won't do it on foot. No horse has, as yet, left and come into Mafeking since the end of October last year, and this is rather a perilous adventure. He took my new charger and a few packets of letters, and started for Vryburg. I accompanied him up to the outside forts, which are just within a stone's throw of the Boer lines, to listen if they would fire at him. So I left here with him at 7.00 o'clock. We rode and rode to the south of the Stadt, but could not find any Forts. Jacob [74] told me that we had passed them, and were already within disputed territory, but I thought he was merely fooling. He even told me he would rather tell me to return and go on himself, but he cannot do so as he must see the Advanced Guards for guidance, so we came back homeward, much against my will. We came along a broad road and to our surprise, after riding a long distance, we observed a fort in front of us – we had passed it about half a mile [back]. When we got there the fellows were all game, and imagining that we were Boers, had their rifles ready cocked – about 6 or 7 on each of us. They waited until we were within 10 yards of the fort, then challenged us. They recognised our voices and came out to meet us. They sent us to 'Teacher's' fort [75] with a guide and there Rojane received his final injunctions and left us at 3.50. I remained there listening attentively for any fire that could be heard at Jacob. He was only 15 minutes away when the fellows all said he was through, but I strained and listened for another 70 minutes – when I was cocksure of his safe departure. By the time I left they were all confident that he had already passed Madibe. During the time I spent at the fort there was a discussion as to whether he [76] is going to accelerate or relax the progress of the Troops, and the debate turned in favour of the latter thought. Rojane is a brave man, no mistake! He was the first D.R. [77] who ever left Mafeking, on October 14th. After this, matters became so serious that no horse could cross the Boers round Mafeking for over 4 months, and he again is the first to venture out on horse back.

### Thursday, 29th

Another very quiet day. 'Au Sanna' never fired a shot today. Emang has left our mess in obedience to maternal instruction.

Today, before the Summary Jurisdiction Court, a Shangaan was charged with the theft of a horse. The prisoner pleaded something equivalent to 'guilty under provocation'. He had been living on 'thepe'.[78] This is partly wholesome as long as it is green, but it becomes bitter and indigestible as soon as the sun's rays affect it. We have not had rain for 10 days; and the heat is so intense that 5 days without rain dries the grass completely and our friend's plea was therefore justifiable. The man could have been convicted if it were not for Col. Hore. He always views things in the same light, and often makes as sarcastic remarks [as] the Supreme Court Judges. When his brother justice was about to find the man guilty, he said: 'The soup kitchen people are entirely to blame for these shameful deeds. Just look at him: his two legs are scarcely able to hold the fellow's body. They don't feed the people at all.'

He wouldn't agree to any verdict and it was decided his case would wait until the soup kitchen affair had been investigated.

Mr Bell issues free tickets to people without means and they always come to say that they do not get any soup although they had the ticket.

Old Tshipithata simply died suddenly this morning. He was a bit sickly and the illness increased during last week when he was out cattle raiding.

*Friday, 30th*

We are having abnormally quiet days lately.

The Colonel Commanding has published a hot protest against alleged rumours by somebodies,[79] to the effect that he delays the troops and that he starves the inhabitants, etc., in the *Mafeking Mail*. He threatens to catch those fellows when their claims [prove false].[80]

### THE COLONEL ON 'GROUSING'.

I hear that again wiseacres are busy in town, informing people as to what I am doing and what I am leaving undone. As their deductions are somewhat inaccurate I wish to state that the condition of affairs is in no way altered since my last general notice, which stated we must be prepared to remain besieged all that time. Indeed I hope that we may be free within the next fortnight or three weeks, but it would be folly on our part not to be prepared against possible unforeseen delays. Had we not been thus prepared in the first instance we should all have been prisoners in Pretoria by the beginning of January, and the Boers would have now been enjoying the use of our property in Mafeking.

I am, I suppose, the most anxious of anybody in Mafeking to see a Relief Column here and the siege at an end; all that can be done for our relief, from both North and South, is being done, but the moves of troops in the face of the enemy must necessarily be slow, and we have to sit in patience until they develop.

As regards the smallness of our rations, we could, of course, live well on full rations for a week or two and then give in to the 'women slaughterers' and let them take their vengeance on the town, whereas by limiting our amount of daily food we can make certain of outlasting all their efforts against us. The present ration, properly utilised, is a fairly full one as compared with those issued in other sieges – in fact I and my staff have, during the past few days, been living on a far smaller ration without any kind of extras to improve it – and we still live.

There are, by the way, two hints I should like to give for making small rations go further – hints derived from personal experience of previous hungry times – and these are:

1. To lump your rations together as much as possible for cooking, and not every man to have his little amount cooked separately.

2. To make the whole into a big thick stew, from which, even three quarter lbs. of ingredients per man, three good meals can be got per day.

It is just possible that we may have to take 2 ozs. off the bread stuffs, but otherwise our supplies will last well over the period indicated. It has been objected that we are feeding horses on oats, but the oats so used are a lot (of Colonial oats) that have been found quite useless for making flour from or human consumption.

I am told that I keep back news from the public. This is not in accordance with facts, for I make a point of publishing all news of general interest as soon as possible after receipt, first by telephone, then by notices posted about, and lastly through Mr Whales, in the Mafeking Mail Slips; I have no object whatever in keeping news back. Occasionally, of course, items of military information have to be kept quiet because, as we all know, their publication in Mafeking means their transmission within a few hours, to the enemy's camp.

Although it may have been somewhat out of my province, I have been writing to the High Commissioner as strongly as I could put them, the claims which the citizens and refugees have for consideration in the matter of compensation, pressing for very early settlement on some more satisfactory basis than was the case on a former occasion. And there is no doubt that the good part they have borne in the defence of the place will add great force to their claims.

I have no feeling of doubt whatever that the large majority of the townspeople have sufficient confidence in me to know that I am working, as far as possible, for their good, but there are always busybodies in every assemblage to cavil at whatever is done, and I should like just to remind these gentlemen of the order issued early in the siege about 'grousing'.

I am always, not only willing, but anxious to personally hear any reasonable complaints or suggestions, and those who have them to make, need only bring their grievances to me to get what redress is in my power, but veiled hints and growlings cannot be permitted; at such times as these they are apt to put people 'on edge' and to alarm the ladies, and for these reasons they must be suppressed. 'Grousing' is generally the outcome of funk on the part of the individual who grouses, and I hope that every right-minded man who hears any of it will shut it up with an appropriate remark, or the toe of his boot. Cavillers should keep quiet until the siege is over and then they are welcome to write or talk until they are blue in the face.

By these remarks I do not wish for one instant to suggest that this 'grousing' is widespread. On the contrary the patience and loyal obedience of the main body of the inhabitants under the restrictions of Martial Law, form one of the conspicuous features of the siege. But there are a few individual grumblers − most of whom are known to me (as they will find when their claims for compensation come up for adjudication) − and it is these gentlemen that I desire to warn to keep quiet as otherwise I shall have to take more stringent steps against them, but I should be ashamed if the fame of Mafeking and its heroic defence should be marred by any whisper among envious outsiders, that there was any want of harmony or unity of purpose among us.

R. S. S. BADEN-POWELL,
Colonel.

EDITORIAL NOTE

The despair of February was not to continue through March. The arrival of encouraging news and hopes of impending relief contributed to the raising of morale. Petty crime increased noticeably, however, probably due to the growing shortage of food. For example, Captain Greener, the Chief Paymaster, was to warn the public of attempts to exchange counterfeit coupons. Yet successive reports of Boer defeats continued to raise the hopes of the beleaguered populace. The *Mafeking Mail* of 13 March reflected the general view in its headline 'The End in Sight'. The Boer artillery, conspicuously silent during the first half of the month, did nothing to dispel rising hopes. The fact that the lines of investment were proving easier to cross was also interpreted as an encouraging sign.

The food situation was, however, rapidly degenerating, and it was in this regard that the Barolong cattle-raiders made a notable contribution. Retrospective analysis has tended to ignore the rôle of Mathakgong and his compatriots in the survival of the besieged population. Plaatje's figures (seemingly accurate in this respect) indicate that these raiders not only brought in loot when it was needed, but also acted as a guerrilla force.

In the *stadt*, where the injection of hope was hardly felt, starvation was a more urgent issue. Here it was no longer a matter of discomfort, but of life or death. The cause of these desperate Barolong was taken up by certain of the townspeople who felt that the African food-situation demanded a moral decision. But this campaign failed, as the military authorities stood firmly behind the prevailing arrangements. Apologists for Baden-Powell (of whom Grinnell-Milne is perhaps the most ardent) claim that the 'obvious answer' was that the garrison would have been 'starved into surrender within two weeks' – and, that in the hands of the Boers, the Barolong would not have fared well.[81] The validity of this speculation, is, however, questionable.

It is not only in respect of the 'Native Question' that the Commanding Officer was, for the first time, being criticised. There were persistent rumours that Baden-Powell wished to prolong the siege, thereby causing unnecessary hardship to the population. The threat to morale that this gossip was posing prompted Baden-Powell's letter of denial at the end of the month. Also, the garrison emphasised that, on the military front, significant progress was being made. The capture of trenches in the brickfields and successes in the artillery duels were enthusiastically reported in the *Mafeking Mail*.

As Plaatje's entries for this month reflect, there was a widespread belief within the lines of investment that relief was imminent. This is perhaps why the criticism and the gossip gained no real ground among the civilians. But relief was, in fact, almost six weeks off, and during this final period the people of Mafeking were to be tested more seriously than they had been before.

CHAPTER NOTES

1 Plaatje began work in the Kimberley Post Office seven years before. 'Service' refers to the Cape Civil Service.
2 From here to the end of the day's entry the text is in shorthand.
3 From here to the end of the day's entry the text is in shorthand.
4 Sergeant-Major William Ashton Taylor, of the Colonial Contingent.
5 From here until the end of the day's entry shorthand has been used. This switch from longhand to shorthand, soon after the start of an entry, seems to have been occasioned by haste.
6 Cape Police.
7 See 27 February. In that context it is spelt 'Mapachwe'.
8 Tswana (properly *moretlhwa*): 'a bush bearing edible brown berries'. (Sotho: 'the plant *Grewia occidentalis* or four corners, *kruisbessie*'. See T. J. Kriel, *New English-Sesotho Dictionary*, 1958.) Phrased thus, it is intended to indicate that the boy had been eating the berries.

9 I.e., the boy that Plaatje met.

10 A town on the Modder River, near Kimberley, but in the Orange Free State.

11 The entries for the next two days are written in shorthand.

12 I.e., 'Cape Boys', the coloured half-breed contingent then under the command of Sergeant Currie. Literally, the appellation means 'Cape people' (Dutch).

13 On 1 March the *Mafeking Mail* noted: 'A letter has been sent to General Snyman by the Colonel Commanding to the following effect: "That as General Snyman has used armed Natives for the invasion of our territory, and is employing them directly against us, the Colonel proposed to act in a similar manner." ' Snyman probably wished intelligence to filter back to Mafeking to the effect that these men had now been disarmed – implying that the O.C. should follow suit. Information implanted in this manner stood a far greater chance of being believed than did an official letter.

14 A rumour had circulated that the Boers were preparing to leave and had placed a dummy in 'Sanna's' position as a ruse. The fact that the barrel was, on several occasions, elevated without the gun being fired added to the widespread conviction. The rumour was dispelled the following day.

15 Ben Weil.

16 See notes to the entry for Tuesday, 27 February.

17 This epigrammatic format was used by the *Mafeking Mail* ('Special Edition' of 8 March) to herald this news.

18 The English Press at the time consistently referred to the Boers as 'women slayers'. Incidents in which women and children, both within and outside the *laagers*, had allegedly been fired upon by the enemy were seized upon to substantiate this view.

19 I.e., his generalship is at an end.

20 The Barolong Boo Rapulana, at Lotlhakane (Rietfontein).

21 Lobatse lies forty-seven miles north of Mafeking in Botswana (then the Bechuanaland Protectorate).

22 There is no previous mention of them.

23 Madibe Siding is approximately ten miles to the south-west of Mafeking and lies in Tshidi-Barolong territory.

24 This farm lies approximately seventeen miles south-south-west of Mafeking (and eight miles south of Madibe).

25 Tswana: 'Restrain them [the cattle], let us fight for them [the cattle]. They laugh and say, We are young boys of writing who are not able to defend ourselves. These Boers, even the English are accustomed to hand over everything of ours. They want them [the cattle] standing [and] us to fight for them.' The meaning of the first sentence is clear. By the second, Mathakgong means that the Boers laugh at them, saying that because they are literate (Barolong, among tribes in the area, being thought of as having a high level of literacy and of being inept in battle), they are weak. He continues to imply that the English were used to conceding Barolong interests in the face of Boer demands – a view that was gaining support among some Barolong at the time.

26 I.e., on the raid. No information could be obtained concerning this man.

27 See the entry for 6 November.

28 Captain Marsh (Royal West Kent Regiment) commanded a squadron of the Protectorate Regiment.

29 A village five miles north-west of Mafeking.

30 See note 62 to entry of 25 February.

31 Only one siege survivor could recall these names, and could provide no more information than that they were foreigners who lived in the location.

32 Or Bodibe, about twenty miles south-east of Mafeking.

33 Dutch: 'Here are the Kaffirs.'
34 Civil Commissioner and Resident Magistrate (C. G. H. Bell.)
35 Sotho: 'We are frightened by roaring only.' Presumably Plaatje intends that they had overestimated Boer strength in that area; it was their 'roaring' (perhaps gunfire) that gave the impression they were numerous.
36 This refers to the Rapulana-Barolong who were Boer allies.
37 In the *stadt*.
38 Notice of this order was first served by Lord E. M. Cecil in the *Mafeking Mail*, 19 February 1900.
39 'Gun' was probably the nickname for the husband or son of Mrs (the wife of) Titshala.
40 See entry for 10 February 1900.
41 A friend of Plaatje's, living near Setlagoli. The name should be contracted into one word and not written as two.
42 This Barolong boo Ratlou village lies approximately forty-eight miles southwest of Mafeking.
43 The 'Big Hole' of Kimberley.
44 Sotho-Tswana (in combination): 'They will hate one another.' This sentence is puzzling in this context for, despite the punctuation, it is not clear how it relates to the preceding lines. Perhaps it is intended to refer to the Boer prisoners and their captors.
45 Tswana: literally, 'Die having conquered for yourself.' *Ikaletse* (past applicative) here should be spelt *ikhaletse*; this omission could be a function of the orthographic confusion of that era.
46 The mission station and diamond-digging centre near Barkly West, Cape Province, where Plaatje received much of his education.
47 I.e., Barkly West.
48 Reverend Westphal of the Lutheran Mission at Pniel was Plaatje's teacher at the mission school.
49 Henry Burton, South African politician and statesman. He was admitted to the Bar in 1892 and thereafter practised in Kimberley. After the Jameson Raid he became a strong supporter of the Afrikander Bond. Burton was elected to Parliament in 1902. He later became Attorney-General and held the ministries of Native Affairs, Railways and Finance during his career.
50 I.e., the relief troops.
51 Dutch: 'Shelter'.
52 Margin note here reads: 'Heard in the Court of Summary Jurisdiction on Monday, March 19th, before His Hon., Maj. H. J. Goold-Adams and Lt.-Col. Hore.'
53 I.e., Shangaan.
54 I.e., Bechuanalander.
55 Dutch: 'thin', 'emaciated'.
56 The outer area of the *stadt*.
57 A railway cottage five miles from Mafeking on the line to the south known as 5 Mile Cottage.
58 Sotho-Tswana; correctly, *ngwan'a molimo* (a contraction of *ngwana a molimo*), it means (literally) 'child of god' or 'young god'. The English 's is obviously meant to replace the Sotho-Tswana possessive, despite the fact that it is written in the wrong place.
59 Dutch: 'shepherd'.
60 Sotho: 'guide'. (The Tswana equivalent is *moshup watsela*.) As his is a common name, the guide concerned could not be identified.

61 There are several references to this man, but Plaatje gives no further clue as to his identity.

62 Sotho-Tswana: 'ruins'.

63 Macheng Pan lies to the east of a Barolong Farm, Oxpan, in Botswana. It is (as the crow flies) twenty-eight miles north-west of Mafeking.

64 This is a Batlharo village twenty miles north-west of Mafeking.

65 Although there is a full stop after the word, it appears that Plaatje had intended to continue. Tshipithata is the name of a man mentioned both before and after this entry; although the word (or rather two words – *tshipi* and *thatha*) has meaning outside this naming context, it would not be applicable here.

66 On this day there were more shells fired at Mafeking than on any other during the siege.

67 I.e., the Court of Summary Jurisdiction.

68 *Mafeking Mail*, 27 March: 'Corroboration has been received from several sources that relief, from the south, is now well this side of Vryburg.'

69 In fact they did read it that day.

70 I.e., for not having told his brother-in-law, Bud Mbelle.

71 Xhosa: 'This man wants to buy a horse at £15, but he is waiting for me to arrive.'

72 Xhosa: 'Therefore he went with it [i.e. the horse] to town and I never did see it.' *Edolopene* is wrongly spelt, it should read *edolophini*.

73 Obviously a case heard at the Court of Summary Jurisdiction some time before.

74 I.e., Rojane.

75 This must have been Plaatje's nickname for an established perimeter-fort. It is not mentioned in any other siege-document.

76 Baden-Powell.

77 Dispatch Rider.

78 Tswana: 'A species of vegetable with a spinach flavour.'

79 This style of expression is a result of direct translation from Setswana. It is frequently heard among present-day Barolong.

80 As this letter is an important indicator of the situation at the time when Plaatje chose to discontinue his entries, it has been decided to reproduce it in full (*Mafeking Mail*, 29 March). After this last entry there is a copy of a letter obviously written some time before. Because its content is not relevant to the diary itself, it has been omitted.

81 Grinnell-Milne, *Baden-Powell at Mafeking*, p. 179.

# EPILOGUE

A review of the day-to-day reports compiled during the siege conveys the impression that the first twenty-three days in April were, in most respects, unremarkable. There was little fighting of any description, though shelling reached a climax on the 11th. After that day 'Au Sanna' fired no more, as the siege-gun was transferred to Pretoria. Only the briefest of skirmishes punctuated the endurance test which the siege had become. Ammunition in Mafeking was in short supply, and the garrison had no desire to waste it on fruitless artillery-duels. Furthermore, Baden-Powell received a communication from Lord Roberts on the 20th stating that Mafeking would not be relieved by the 18 May, as had been intended. The food situation was, of course, serious, although locusts provided yet another source – especially for the Barolong in the *stadt*. The month of April, as recounted in the *Mafeking Mail*, was one of minor events arranged by the military leadership to allay the anxieties of the citizenry.

The 24th, however, marked the start of a new phase in the confrontation. On that day Sarel Eloff, the grandson of Paul Kruger, returned to Mafeking from Pretoria with reinforcements and a firm resolve to breach the six-month-old defences. The garrison expected an attack immediately after his return; but the previous pattern of intermittent shelling continued, and the month of May had a relatively quiet beginning.

The Sunday truce, which had been effectively honoured by both sides despite the odd misunderstanding and occasional threats, was broken on the first sabbath of the month. Heavy shelling provided a cover for a Boer raiding-party which successfully made off with a number of horses. Again the garrison expected an attack; and again nothing happened – at least, not for six days. On the 12th, Eloff mounted what turned out to be the final attempt to overrun Mafeking by direct onslaught.

Before dawn the town received heavy fire from the east. While the garrison prepared itself for the attack, and tried to anticipate the direction from which it would come, Eloff and his 250 men crept quietly along the Molopo in the direction of the *stadt*. Guided by a British deserter who was familiar with the perimeter defences and their weaknesses, the Boer party intended to force its way into the town. As soon as this had been accomplished, reinforcements led by Snyman were to have completed the defeat of Mafeking. Eloff sent word to a Reuter correspondent that, at a given signal from the *stadt*, he should publish the news of the 'fall'.

Under cover of darkness they advanced stealthily into the maze of huts. Once Eloff had led his men away from the river in the direction of the British South African Police Camp, he signalled his triumph. The thatched roof of a hut was ignited and spectacular flames heralded the start of a lively battle. Soon the conflagration spread and a chaotic stampede to safety on the part of the Barolong obscured – and hence facilitated – the execution of a pincer movement towards the Camp. In the meantime, the Boer forces supported the advance with rifle-fire – but the offensive which General Snyman had promised to lead never materialised.

Eloff reached the B.S.A.P. Camp and found it manned by sixteen soldiers of the Protectorate Regiment under Colonel Hore. The attacking party imprisoned these soldiers in the fort at the centre of the camp and proceeded to assume positions in the outbuildings. But, in the absence of support, the Boers soon found themselves isolated. One French volunteer who had accompanied Eloff climbed onto the roof of the fort with a bottle of Burgundy from the captured officers' mess and drank a toast to 'Fashoda'. But he received only satirical comment from the surrounding British – and a sniper's bullet through the heart. The garrison had organised itself very rapidly, and effected an 'investment-within-an-investment' with parade-ground precision. The stragglers that Eloff left behind him in the *stadt* were either killed or forced to beat a hasty retreat to their own lines.

Throughout the day the intrepid young Boer Commander held the fort. But, in the absence of water – for the supply tank had been destroyed by British rifle-fire – and reinforcement, many of Eloff's men chose to attempt an escape into the protective trees of the Molopo. By six o'clock in the evening Eloff was left no choice but to surrender to Colonel Hore. After a cease-fire had been arranged, Baden-Powell met the prisoners at the Market Square. Eloff had been convinced of his ability to take Mafeking in the half-light of dawn. 'Breakfast at Dixon's' had been his rallying cry. He had arrived under slightly different circumstances – for dinner. The officers of the beleaguered garrison were unanimous in the view that, despite his ultimate failure, the young officer had earned the meal with his display of courage.

The 'Fall of Mafeking' was reported as arranged and caused predictable feelings of joy and despair. In fact, the truth differed radically from the intelligence contained in the Reuter correspondent's dispatch. On 16 May Colonel Mahon's relief-force from the south met Plumer approximately nineteen miles outside Mafeking. Fighting their way through, the combined party reached the outskirts of the town and paused to rest before effecting the relief before dawn the next day. They met little opposition from Snyman's weary soldiers and marched triumphantly into the market square on the seventeenth of the month.

So ended the siege of Mafeking. The daily rigours of the previous months gave way to ceremony and celebration. Baden-Powell and many members of the garrison left for new theatres of war. Citizens who had been evacuated to safety in October began to return by the restored rail-service; community-life in the town slowly returned to normal.

In the *stadt* the tribesmen listened proudly to tributes paid to their bravery and resilience.[1] In return, they pledged their unswerving loyalty to His Majesty and the Imperial government. The 'foreign' Africans of the Black Watch and other contingents were promised a farm as a collective reward. They never received it. The Barolong were assured of British political protection from the Boers in reciprocation for their part in the alliance. They, too, were later to feel more than a little dissatisfied with British breach of promise.[2] In the meantime, however, like everyone else, they were left to salve their wounds in peace.

EPILOGUE NOTES

1 For a full account of events in the *stadt* directly after the relief, see Molema, *The Bantu, Past and Present*; Plaatje, *Native Life in South Africa*.
2 For a discussion of British policy in South Africa concerning the protection of African interests see Plaatje, *Native Life in South Africa*.

# BIBLIOGRAPHY

Agar-Hamilton, J. A. I., *The Road to the North. South Africa 1852–1886* (London: Longmans, 1937).

Baillie, Major F. D., *Mafeking: a Diary of the Siege* (London: Constable, 1900).

Breutz, P.-L., *The Tribes of the Mafeking District*, Department of Native Affairs Ethnological Publication no. 32 (Pretoria, 1956).

Cowen, V., 'Diary of the Siege of Mafeking'. Unpublished MS.

Gardiner, B., *Mafeking: a Victorian Legend* (London: Cassell, 1966).

Grinnell-Milne, D., *Baden-Powell at Mafeking* (London: Bodley Head, 1957).

Hamilton, J. A., *The Siege of Mafeking* (London: Methuen, 1900).

Kuper, A., *Kalahari Village Politics: an African Democracy*, Cambridge Studies in Social Anthropology no. 3 (London: Cambridge University Press, 1970).

Mackenzie, J., *Austral Africa: Losing It or Ruling It* (London: Sampson Low, 1887).

Matthews, Z. K., 'A Short History of the Tshidi-Barolong', in *Fort Hare Papers*, vol. I, no. 1 (1945).

Molema, S. M., *The Bantu Past and Present* (Cape Town: Struik, 1963). This is a facsimile reprint of the 1920 edition published in Edinburgh by Green & Son.

—, *Montshiwa: Barolong Chief and Patriot* (Cape Town: Struik, 1966).

Plaatje, S. T., *Native Life in South Africa* (New York: The Crisis, n.d., believed to be 1916).

—, *Mhudi: an Epic of South African Native Life a Hundred Years Ago* (Alice: Lovedale Press, 1957). No earlier edition could be located.

Schapera, I., *A Handbook of Tswana Law and Custom* (London: International Institute of African Languages and Culture, 1938).

—, 'The System of Land Tenure on the Barolong Farms'. Unpublished report to the Bechuanaland Protectorate Government, 1943.

—, *The Tswana* (London: Sidney Press, for the International African Institute Ethnographic Survey of Africa, 1953).

Sillery, A., *The Bechuanaland Protectorate* (Cape Town: Oxford University Press, 1952).

Stanislaus, Mother M., 'Diary of the Siege of Mafeking'. Unpublished MS.

Young, F., *The Relief of Mafeking* (London: Methuen, 1900).